Developing Courses in English for Specific

Developing Courses in English for Specific Purposes

Helen Basturkmen

University of Auckland, New Zealand

First published 2010 by
PALGRAVE MACMILLAN

Palgrave Macmillan in the UK is an imprint of Macmillan Publishers Limited,
registered in England, company number 785998, of Houndmills, Basingstoke,
Hampshire RG21 6XS.

Palgrave Macmillan in the US is a division of St Martin's Press LLC,
175 Fifth Avenue, New York, NY 10010.

Palgrave Macmillan is the global academic imprint of the above companies
and has companies and representatives throughout the world.

Palgrave® and Macmillan® are registered trademarks in the United States,
the United Kingdom, Europe and other countries.

ISBN 978–0–230–22797–2   hardback
ISBN 978–0–230–22798–9   paperback

This book is printed on paper suitable for recycling and made from fully
managed and sustained forest sources. Logging, pulping and manufacturing
processes are expected to conform to the environmental regulations of the
country of origin.

A catalogue record for this book is available from the British Library.

Library of Congress Cataloging-in-Publication Data

Basturkmen, Helen.
    Developing courses in English for specific purposes / Helen Basturkmen.
       p. cm.
    Includes bibliographical references and index.
    ISBN 978–0–230–22798–9   (pbk.)
    1. English language—Study and teaching (Higher)—Foreign speakers.   I. Title.
PE1128.A2B316 2010
428.0071'1—dc22
                                                                    2010027488

10   9   8   7   6   5   4   3   2   1
19 18 17 16 15 14 13 12 11 10

Printed and bound in Great Britain by
CPI Antony Rowe, Chippenham and Eastbourne

Contents

List of Figures and Tables		viii
Preface		x
Acknowledgements		xiii
List of Abbreviations		xiv
1	**Introduction**	**1**
	1.1 Describing ESP	1
	1.2 Areas in ESP	3
	1.3 Demands of teaching ESP	7
	1.4 Effectiveness of ESP	9
	1.5 Summary	12
	1.6 Discussion	12
Part I	**Main Considerations in ESP Course Development**	**15**
2	**Analysing Needs**	**17**
	2.1 Introduction	17
	2.2 Definitions of needs analysis	17
	2.3 Hypothetical scenarios	19
	2.4 Needs analysis as a course design process	25
	2.5 Building on existing knowledge	26
	2.6 Types of information to collect	30
	2.7 Summary	34
	2.8 Discussion	34
3	**Investigating Specialist Discourse**	**36**
	3.1 Importance of descriptions of specialist discourse in ESP	36
	3.2 When teachers/course developers conduct investigations	40
	3.3 Approaches to investigation of specialist communication	43
	3.4 Summary	47
	3.5 Discussion	49
4	**Developing the Curriculum**	**52**
	4.1 Focusing the course	52
	4.2 Determining course content	59
	4.3 Developing materials	62

4.4	Evaluating courses and materials	64
4.5	Summary	67
4.6	Discussion	68

Part II   Case Studies in ESP Course Development — 69

5   English for the Police — 71

5.1	Context	71
5.2	Investigating needs	72
5.3	Investigating specialist discourse	74
5.4	Designing the course and materials	76
5.5	Responding to difficulties and constraints	84
5.6	Summary	85
5.7	Discussion	86

6   English for Medical Doctors — 88

6.1	Context	89
6.2	Investigating needs	90
6.3	Investigating specialist discourse	92
6.4	Designing the course and materials	97
6.5	Responding to difficulties and constraints	104
6.6	Summary	105
6.7	Discussion	106

7   Academic Literacies in Visual Communication — 108

7.1	Context	109
7.2	Investigating needs	110
7.3	Investigating specialist discourse	111
7.4	Designing the course and materials	114
7.5	Responding to difficulties and constraints	119
7.6	Summary	120
7.7	Discussion	120

8   English for Thesis Writing — 122

8.1	Context	123
8.2	Investigating needs	124
8.3	Investigating specialist discourse	126
8.4	Designing the workshop series and materials	129
8.5	Responding to difficulties and constraints	131
8.6	Summary	135
8.7	Discussion	135

9   Conclusion   137

   9.1   Revisiting the main considerations in ESP course development   137
   9.2   A visual representation of ESP course development   142
   9.3   Future trends   144
   9.4   Summary   145

References   146

Author Index   152

Subject Index   154

List of Figures and Tables

Figures

1.1	Areas of ESP teaching	6
1.2	ESP course timing in relation to work or study experience of learners	6
1.3	Definition of absolute and variable characteristics of ESP	13
2.1	The role of needs analysis in course design	26
2.2	An example questionnaire used in needs analysis © The American University. Published by Elsevier Ltd	30
2.3	Advantages and disadvantages of questionnaires and interviews	32
4.1	The wide- and narrow-angled continuum	55
4.2	Section from a company annual report as sample authentic text	60
4.3	Simulation activity using authentic texts	60
5.1	Types of needs in policing	74
5.2	Describing 'on the job' and academic language needs © Languages International and New Zealand Police 2008	74
5.3	Course objectives from the English for Police course	76
5.4	Example of self-access, online lesson developed for the English for Police course © Languages International and New Zealand Police 2008	78
5.5	Course structure in the English for Police course	81
5.6	Service station credit card case lesson © Languages International 2009	81
6.1	Introduction to the professional development course for overseas-trained medical doctors. Reprinted with kind permission of Dr Sue Hawken and Dr Richard Fox, School of Medicine, University of Auckland	90
6.2	Criteria in the Observed Consultation Appraisal Form. Reprinted with the kind permission of Dr Rosemary Wette, Department of Applied Language Studies and Linguistics, University of Auckland.	92
6.3	Selection of salient discourse features and illustrative samples of language use. Reprinted with the kind permission of Dr Rosemary Wette, Department of Applied Language Studies and Linguistics, University of Auckland	96

6.4   Observed Consultation Appraisal Form. Reprinted with the
      kind permission of Dr Rosemary Wette, Department of Applied
      Language Studies and Linguistics, University of Auckland, and
      Dr Sue Hawkin and Dr Richard Fox, School of Medicine, University
      of Auckland   99

6.5   Content page from the overseas-trained doctors' English language
      classes. Reprinted with the kind permission of Dr Rosemary
      Wette, Department of Applied Language Studies and Linguistics,
      University of Auckland   101

6.6   Instructional strategy for the overseas-trained doctors' classes   101

6.7   Sample error-correction activity. Reprinted with the kind
      permission of Dr Rosemary Wette, Department of Applied
      Language Studies and Linguistics, University of Auckland   102

6.8   Drawing students' attention to features of language use and
      communication skills. Reprinted with the kind permission of
      Dr Rosemary Wette, Department of Applied Language Studies and
      Linguistics, University of Auckland   103

6.9   Observing formulaic expressions. Reprinted with the
      kind permission of Dr Rosemary Wette, Department of Applied
      Language Studies and Linguistics, University of Auckland   104

7.1   Text from the ALVC course handbook © AUT University Auckland   112

7.2   Part of the ALVC course outline © AUT University Auckland   115

7.3   Course material on structures of critical writing © AUT University
      Auckland   117

8.1   Content and organization of the Discussion of Results   127

8.2   Examples of hedges   128

8.3   Interview questions for supervisors   129

8.4   Workshop series: Outline of content © AUT University Auckland   130

8.5   Sample material from the literature review workshop
      © AUT University Auckland   132

9.1   Representation of ESP course development   143

Tables

3.1   Concordances from semantic category of 'research'   48

3.2   Words from semantic category of 'research'   49

4.1   Examples of 'Communication in Science' topics © *English for
      Specific Purposes*, 26 (4). Published by Elsevier Ltd   62

Preface

Aims and audience

This book is about how ESP courses are developed and designed. It aims to make the topic of ESP course development as accessible as possible to a wide audience of teachers and prospective teachers, and to show how ideas about course development in the literature can be related to practice. The book describes the considerations ESP teachers and course developers take into account in their work. It introduces the reader to three major aspects of ESP course design (analysing needs, investigating specialist discourse and determining the curriculum). The work presents case studies and discusses them in relation to issues and considerations in these three areas.

The book targets practice and has a 'how to do it' type orientation. It focuses on course design – how to design an ESP course and how did experienced ESP teachers set about developing courses. The work is premised on the idea that we can learn a good deal from observing experienced teachers/course developers (observing how they set about developing courses, the kinds of decisions they make and how they respond to practical difficulties) as well as from the literature.

The book will be of interest to participants on undergraduate or postgraduate programmes in TESOL. It will be of interest also to practising teachers, either those already working in ESP or who envisage teaching ESP in the future.

Content and organization

The book has two main parts. Part I introduces the reader to three important areas of ESP course design – needs analysis, investigation of specialist discourse and curriculum planning. Part II presents four ESP case studies. Each case is discussed in relation to decisions made and how the ESP course developers set about analysing needs, investigating specialist discourse and determining the curriculum. The chapters in the main body of the work end with discussion questions. The questions encourage the reader to draw on the concepts introduced in the chapter in examining their own experiences and views of teaching and learning, investigating ESP courses in their own environments or developing small-scale projects.

Part I

Chapter 1 introduces ESP by examining definitions of ESP and the different areas of work involved (such as English for Academic Purposes and English for Professional Purposes). It considers the demands that teaching and developing

ESP courses make on the teacher and thus paves the way for the book, which aims to provide teachers with the relevant knowledge and skills for these tasks. Finally, the chapter considers how ESP teaching promotes learning.

Chapters 2, 3 and 4 examine key areas in ESP course development. Chapter 2 focuses on Needs Analysis and highlights its importance in ESP. The chapter describes the types of needs that are investigated and the role of needs analysis in the course design process. The chapter makes suggestions for how teachers and course developers can set about investigating needs and describes the types of information that are collected. The chapter also describes ways teachers and course developers can make use of published needs analyses. Chapter 3 focuses on Investigating Specialist Discourse. The chapter considers the importance of descriptions of specialist discourse in teaching ESP. It discusses the circumstances in which course developers need to conduct their own investigations and shows ways this can be done. The chapter also makes suggestions for when and how teachers and course developers can track down and make use of published descriptions of specialist discourse. Chapter 4 examines the kinds of decisions teachers and course developers make in designing a curriculum and developing materials. It discusses when and why wide- and narrow-angled ESP courses are developed and how the results of a needs analysis can be used in determining the curriculum.

Part II

The chapters in Part II each present a case study of a different ESP course. The courses were developed by highly experienced ESP teachers/course developers (the course developers also taught the courses they developed) and are widely different. Two cases report the development of work-related ESP courses. One case concerns the development of an English course developed for prospective police recruits in a private language school and the second case concerns a course developed for overseas-trained medical doctors. Two cases report the development of study-related courses, one for students on a foundation course in visual arts (students at the very beginning of their university studies) and one for students writing their thesis reports (students towards the very end of their university studies). The cases also differ in regard to the focus of instruction. The English for Police course was developed to focus on a number of communicative events in policing whereas the English for Medical Doctors course focused on just one event in medical practice (the patient-centred medical consultation). The third case report traces the development of a course that focused on the needs of students in one discipline (visual arts) and combines language instruction with disciplinary content. The English for Thesis Writing workshop series described in the final case study focuses on needs of students across disciplines. But, as the reader will see, the courses differed in other respects as well.

Each case study chapter follows the same organization. These chapters first describe the context in which the course emerged and then go on to focus on the decisions taken by the teachers/course developers with regard to the three areas of ESP course design examined in Part I (needs analysis, investigating specialist discourse and determining the curriculum). The case studies address the following questions:

Why and how did the course come to be established?

How did the teachers/course developers analyse and define needs?

How did they investigate and describe specialist discourse?

How did they determine the curriculum and incorporate findings from the investigation of needs analysis and specialist discourse?

What are the distinguishing features of the course? (sample materials are used to illustrate)

What constraints and difficulties were involved in developing the course and how did the teachers/course developers respond?

Chapter 9 concludes the work by reflecting on the three main considerations in ESP course development (needs analysis, investigating specialist discourse and determining the curriculum). The chapter considers what can be learnt from the case studies in the three key areas, offers a visual representation of ESP course development and identifies trends in the field.

Acknowledgements

I would like to acknowledge the generous contribution made by the teachers/ course developers who allowed me to interview them, discuss with them and examine the courses and materials they developed for the purposes of the case studies in this book. For their time and generosity in providing information and sharing their expertise, I wish to thank Nick Moore and Peter Nicolls of Languages International, Auckland, Rosemary Wette of the University of Auckland, and Darryl Hocking and John Bitchener of AUT University, Auckland. This book would not have been possible without their help. I would also like to acknowledge the generous support of the teachers/course developers' respective institutions for allowing the cases to be reported in this book. I am grateful to the authors and others who have given their permission to use the material in this book: Languages International Ltd, Auckland, Gary Allcock of the New Zealand Police, Sue Hawkins and Richard Fox from Auckland University School of Medicine, Sharon Harvey from AUT University and Katherine Ciao. My thanks go to my colleagues in the Department of Applied Language Studies and Linguistics at the University of Auckland for their support and to Jenny Jones for her careful attention to detail in proofreading the draft of this book. I am very grateful to Priyanka Gibbons, Melanie Blair and the editorial team at Palgrave Macmillan for their clear advice and work in supporting the development and production of this book. They have been pleasant and helpful to work with.

The publisher and I are grateful to the authors and publishers who have given permission to reproduce copyright material. Reprinted from *English for Specific Purposes*, 27 (1) Bacha, N. N. and Bahous, R. 'Contrasting Views of Business Students' Writing Needs in an EFL Environment', pp. 74–93 © 2008 with permission from Elsevier. Reprinted from *English for Specific Purposes*, 26 (4) Parkinson, J., Jackson, L., Kirkwood, T. and Padayachee, V. 'A Scaffolded Reading and Writing Course for Foundation Level Students', pp. 443–61 © 2007 with permission from Elsevier. *Fletcher Building Annual Report 2009* reprinted with permission of Philip King on behalf of Fletcher Building Ltd. Reprinted course materials developed by Nick Moore and Peter Nicolls © Languages International 2009 with permission of the authors. Reprinted course materials developed by Rosemary Wette © University of Auckland with permission of the author. Reprinted course materials developed by Darryl Hocking © AUT University, Auckland with permission of the author. Reprinted course materials developed by John Bitchener © AUT University, Auckland with permission of the author.

List of Abbreviations

EAP	English for Academic Purposes
EGAP	English for General Academic Purposes
ESAP	English for Specific Academic Purposes
EGP	English for General Purposes
ELT	English Language Teaching
EOP	English for Occupational Purposes
EGOP	English for General Occupational Purposes
ESOP	English for Specific Occupational Purposes
EPP	English for Professional Purposes
EGPP	English for General Professional Purposes
ESPP	English for Specific Professional Purposes
ESOL	English for Speakers of Other Languages
ESP	English for Specific Purposes
EST	English for Science and Technology
TESOL	Teaching English to Speakers of Other Languages

1
Introduction

This chapter is organized into four sections. The first section considers how different writers have described English for Specific Purposes (ESP) and identifies common themes. The second surveys areas of ESP teaching and offers a categorization. The third discusses the work of ESP teachers and the particular demands ESP teaching and course design can make on them. The final section considers ideas about the effectiveness of ESP courses with reference to empirical evidence provided by research and theoretical arguments.

1.1 Describing ESP

This section considers the question 'What is ESP teaching?'

What do you understand by the term 'ESP teaching'?

The boxes below contain a selection of statements about ESP teaching by various writers. The terms 'English Language Teaching' (ELT) and 'English for General Purposes' (EGP) are used. A number of themes can be seen in these statements.

Box 1.1

The basic insight that language can be thought of as a tool for communication rather than as sets of phonological, grammatical and lexical items to be memorized led to the notion of developing learning programs to reflect the different communicative needs of disparate groups of learners. No longer was it necessary to teach an item simply because it is 'there' in the language. A potential tourist to England should not have to take the same course as an air traffic controller in Singapore or a Columbian engineer preparing for graduate

1

study in the United States. This insight led to the emergence of English for Specific Purposes (ESP) as an important subcomponent of language teaching, with its own approaches to curriculum development, materials design, pedagogy, testing and research.

Nunan (2004, p. 7)

Box 1.2

If ESP has sometimes moved away from trends in general ELT, it has always retained its emphasis on practical outcomes. We will see that the main concerns of ESP have always been, and remain, with needs analysis, text analysis, and preparing learners to communicate effectively in the tasks prescribed by their study or work situation.

Dudley-Evans and St John (1998, p. 1)

Box 1.3

ESP and General English

It is in the nature of a language syllabus to be selective. The General English syllabus is based on a conception of the kind of reality that the student has to deal with in English. For example, a General English course for teenagers will probably be written around the language-based activities of a stereotypical teenager. Finding out or even speculating on what these activities are is like taking the first step towards a needs analysis. Consciously or unconsciously, therefore, all sensible course designers must begin by trying to assess students' specific needs. ESP is simply a narrowing of this needs spectrum.

The ESP process of specialisation should not result in the complete separation of one part of the language from another. One cannot simply hack off pieces of a language or of skills and then expect them to exist independently of anything else. Every discipline refers to others and each draws on the same reservoir of language. A science student who comes to grips with the past simple passive through the description of laboratory procedures is unlikely to lock that tense into that context for the rest of their English-speaking life.

Holme (1996, pp. 3–4)

Box 1.4

> In fact, the dividing line between ESP and EGP is not always clear; where do we place, for example, a course designed for a Korean businessperson who is to assume a post abroad in the near future? If the learner's proficiency level is very low, a great deal of course content will probably be of a general English type with emphasis on survival situations. Most would probably agree that the course should be classified as ESP, simply because the aims are clearly defined, and analysis of the learner's needs play an important role in deciding what to include in the course. However, we believe our example demonstrates that ESP should not be regarded as a discrete division of ELT, but simply an area (with blurred boundaries) whose courses are usually more focused in their aims and make use of a narrower range of topics.
>
> Barnard and Zemach (2003, pp. 306–7)

One of the common themes in the above statements is that ESP courses are narrower in focus than ELT courses – 'tasks prescribed by their work or study situation' are mentioned in Box 1.2, 'narrowing down the spectrum' in Box 1.3 and 'a narrower range of topics' in Box 1.4. The statements mention learner needs. ESP courses are narrower in focus than general ELT courses because they centre on analysis of learners' needs. The statements show that ESP views learners in terms of their work or study roles and that ESP courses focus on work- or study-related needs, not personal needs or general interests. A number of specific work and study roles were mentioned including an air traffic controller, an engineering student, a science student and a businessperson. And lastly, there is mention of the fact that ESP involves analysis of texts and language use learners will encounter in their work and study situations – 'text analysis' is mentioned in Box 1.2 and 'description of laboratory procedures' in Box 1.4.

These themes are examined in detail in Part I of the book. Chapter 2 examines the role of needs analysis in ESP. Chapter 3 describes investigation into specialist texts and discourse and Chapter 4 examines narrow and wide-angled course designs as one of a set of curriculum design issues in ESP.

1.2   Areas in ESP

ESP teaching takes place in a number of differing contexts as shown in the following scenarios:

1.2.1   Teaching scenarios

1.2.1.1   Alison

Alison began her teaching career teaching French in the secondary school sector in New Zealand. A number of years later due to falling enrolments in European languages in secondary schools, Alison started teaching English as a Second Language in a Tertiary College. She taught intermediate level learners there for some years and then began to also conduct classes for immigrants focusing on 'settling-in skills', such as job applications, dealing with administrative enquiries, and so on. One day her director of studies called her in to tell her that the college was to introduce a course called English for Medical Doctors. The students would be recently arrived immigrant doctors who needed to appear for medical registration examinations and English language tests to enable them to work as general practitioners in the country. Alison was asked to prepare and teach the course.

1.2.1.2   Derya

Derya graduated in teaching English as a foreign language in Turkey and almost immediately gained employment in one of the large state universities in which English is used as the medium of instruction. Most students at Derya's university spend a year in the preparatory school studying an intensive English language programme prior to starting study of subjects in their departments. Derya has taught on the intensive programme for a number of years. Recently, the Engineering faculty at the university expanded its doctoral programme. The faculty however realized that the doctoral students' lack of English was hampering their studies and it was decided that a special English language programme to help the postgraduate students with reading and writing engineering research reports needed to be set up. Derya, whose brother is completing his doctoral studies in the Engineering faculty, was requested to set up a suitable ESP course for the engineering students on the doctoral programme.

1.2.1.3   Albert

Albert is bilingual and was brought up in a French-speaking home in the UK. After studying French and Business at university, during which he did some part-time English for Speakers of Other Languages (ESOL) teaching, he was offered a job with a computer software company based in Paris. His brief was to track the daily work practices of a number of key employees at the company and offer English language assistance to them when they had difficulties using English in their work. The aim was that these key employees should eventually become independent in using English for their workplace needs. At present Albert is tracking and providing language support for one of the company lawyers, whose work involves correspondence with companies in the UK and US, and the head of finance responsible for strategy policy in both the French and UK divisions of the company.

1.2.1.4   Cathy and Louis

Cathy and Louis were completing postgraduate degrees in Teaching English to Speakers of Other Languages (TESOL) when they responded to a job advertisement calling for teachers to work at a military defence training facility in the US. The facility trains military personnel from various countries and aims to improve their technical and English language skills. Cathy and Louis' students were pilots. Having begun teaching at the facility, Cathy and Louis realized that the students' interest in English for its own sake was limited but they were deeply enthusiastic about their specialist areas, such as helicopter piloting. Cathy and Louis quickly set about devising content-based teaching of English in which the primary focus of instruction is on texts and activities related to the students' specialist military areas.

1.2.1.5 John

John studied law at a university in Australia. In his final year he began teaching ESOL part-time in order to supplement his income. He found he enjoyed it more than law and on completing his law degree, he taught ESOL full-time for three years before doing a masters degree in TESOL. For his thesis topic he decided to investigate discourse in 'problem-answer' essays' – an academic legal genre common in legal studies. After receiving his degree, John got a job teaching academic reading and writing skills in the English Language Support centre at an Asian university. Sometime later, he was transferred from the centre to the ESP Unit at the same university in order to work in an established small team that designs and teaches English courses for students in the law department. Here John feels able to combine his interest in language teaching with his knowledge of law and legal discourse.

1.2.1.6 Estelle

Estelle found that after teaching primary school in New Zealand for a number of years, she needed a change of direction. She wanted to work abroad and teach adults. She studied for a diploma in TESOL during which she took a course in ESP. Following her graduation, Estelle found a job in a two-year vocational college. The first course Estelle was assigned to teach was 'English for Office Management'. The course had only been running one year and Estelle was told she would need to prepare new instructional material as there was insufficient course content. The students on this course were between 18 and 20 years old and were hoping to gain employment in international companies after their return to their home countries. Alongside English, the students were studying word processing, spreadsheet and office administration.

The above scenarios illustrate some of the diverse contexts in which ESP teaching takes place. They illustrate the divide between teaching English for Academic Purposes (EAP) – Derya and John (who both work in a university setting and teach English for study-related purposes), teaching English for Professional Purposes (EPP) – Alison, Cathy and Louis and Albert (who teach English to doctors, pilots and company executives respectively), teaching English for Occupational Purposes (EOP) – Estelle (who teaches English for office managers). We see that ESP can be classroom-based, or, as in Albert's situation, on-site workplace-based. The work histories of Derya and John show that they were first involved in teaching English for General Academic Purposes (EGAP) – their work in the Language Preparatory School and Language Support Centre respectively and then were involved in teaching English for Specific Purposes (ESAP). Estelle's teaching experience would be with groups of students who had never worked as office managers (pre-experience ESP), Alison's would be with students who had worked as doctors in their home countries but were not working any more (post-experience ESP), whereas Albert, Cathy and Louis would teach learners who were actually working in their professions at that point in time (during-experience ESP). Figure 1.1 shows the areas of ESP teaching and Figure 1.2 illustrates ESP course timing in relation to the learners' work or study experience.

Branch	Sub Branches	Example
English for Academic Purposes (EAP)	English for General Academic Purposes (EGAP)	English for academic writing
	English for Specific Academic Purposes (ESAP)	English for law studies
English for Professional Purposes (EPP)	English for General Professional Purposes (EGPP)	English for the health care sector
	English for Specific Professional Purposes (ESPP)	English for nursing
English for Occupational Purposes (EOP)	English for General Occupational Purposes (EGOP)	English for the hospitality industry
	English for Specific Occupational Purposes (ESOP)	English for hotel receptionists

Figure 1.1   Areas of ESP teaching

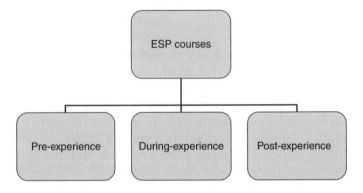

Figure 1.2   ESP course timing in relation to work or study experience of learners

1.3   Demands of teaching ESP

As well as illustrating the diverse areas of ESP teaching, the above scenarios illustrate the demands ESP can pose for teachers. Teachers may find themselves dealing with content in an occupation or subject of study that they themselves have little or no prior knowledge of, as we see in the cases of Derya and Cathy and Louis. Some, such as Albert, may find themselves working alone in an on-site environment. They may find they have far less knowledge and experience in the subject than their learners as in the case of Alison and Albert. In the above scenarios we saw that only John was dealing with a subject he had specialist knowledge in and was working in an experienced team of ESP teachers. Derya had a helpful 'insider-expert' relative to help her understand the situation and needs of her learners, but not all teachers have such contacts. Cathy and Louis were fortunate in working together, but some ESP teachers find themselves working alone without colleagues to 'sound off' ideas for course and materials design.

So how prepared are teachers for teaching what often is a challenging new task? Master (1997a) reviewed the state of ESP teacher education in the US and found that at that time there were no ESP-track MA TESOL programmes although one university was in the process of building one, and a handful of universities had a course in the topic. Howard (1997) surveyed UK universities and found that three offered MA programmes that specialized in ESP and a good number offered a course in the topic. The City University of Hong Kong at this time offers an ESP-track MA and a number of other universities around the world offer MA courses as part of their MA TESOL programmes. However, only some teachers who come to work in ESP have received such formal training. In the above scenarios we saw that ESP was part of the formal professional education of only Estelle and John.

For many ESP teachers, formal TESOL training has been very largely concerned with general ELT. Some might argue that there is little difference between teaching ELT and ESP. Both ELT and ESP share a similar aim – to develop students' communicative competence. Ellis (1996) describes language pedagogy as 'concerned with the ability to use language in communicative situations' (p. 74). Workplace or academic situations can be argued to be simply just some of those situations, a part of the whole. Many ELT courses are based on the principle that language course content should be related to the purposes for which students are expected to use language after all.

Yet there are important differences between teaching general ELT and ESP. Cook (2002) distinguishes between external and internal goals for language teaching. External goals can be related to the uses of language outside the classroom – being able to get things done in the real world, such as being able to buy groceries or provide medical information. Internal goals relate to the educational aims of the classroom – improving attitudes to speakers of other languages, promoting thinking skills such as analysis, memorizing and social goals. ESP teaching is generally understood to be very largely concerned with external goals. In ESP the learner is seen as a language learner engaged either in academic, professional or occupational pursuits and who uses English as a means to carry out those pursuits. External goals suggest an instrumental view of language learning and language being learnt for non-linguistic goals. In a general ELT situation, goals are generally linguistic (such as, development of oral competence or a wide vocabulary, or ability to use a wide range of grammatical structures). In an ESP situation, it is understood that the learner would want to achieve 'real world' objectives, objectives requiring specific linguistic competencies. For example, students on an English-for-nursing course may want to 'complete patient records' appropriately or 'interact with patients' in ways that reduce patients' stress. In this situation, language development is seen as the means to the ends but not as the end in itself, and the learners can easily become de-motivated by language course content that does not appear directly relevant to their real world objectives. The ESP teacher/course developer needs to find out what the language-based objectives of the students are in the target occupation or academic discipline and ensure that the content of the ESP course works towards them.

ESP focuses on when, where and why learners need the language either in study or workplace contexts. Decisions about what to teach, and sometimes how to teach (see Dudley-Evans and St Johns, 1998) are informed by descriptions of how language is used in the particular contexts the learners will work or study in. There is thus a strong focus in ESP on language as 'situated language use'. Although there are exceptions, general ELT tends to focus at least in part on language usage (the underlying systems of the language). This does not mean to say that ESP is exclusively concerned with use and general ELT with usage, it is a matter of degree.

Tudor (1997) points out that an important distinguishing feature of ESP is that it deals with 'domains of knowledge which the average educated native speaker could not reasonably be expected to be familiar with' (p. 91). In other words, what is focused on in ESP courses is not part and parcel of the communicative repertoire of all educated native speakers as in the case of general English teaching. So, for example, in teaching English to a group of nurses, course content might involve items such as medical terminology, patterns of nurse–patient interaction, written genres such as patient records, items that are not in the communicative realm of those outside nursing fields. This distinction also holds in the case of EAP teaching that deals with subject-specific matter, ESAP, such as English for Legal Studies or English for Biology Studies. It does not hold as well in the case of EGAP. The great majority of ESP teachers will themselves be graduates and have considerable experience in academic texts and skills. They are less likely, however, to have conscious knowledge of them. For example, if an EGAP course focuses on academic speaking skills, the teacher may have good ability himself/herself to speak in academic contexts but is likely to have only a tacit understanding of the skills or features of language use involved. To design and teach a course in academic speaking, the teacher will need to have an explicit understanding of those skills, such as presentation and discussion skills. Because of the focus on either an area of knowledge that is outside the communicative repertoire of all educated native speakers or on making explicit skills that educated native speakers have only tacit awareness of, teaching ESP makes additional demands on the teacher. The ESP teacher needs to learn how to design courses in a conceptual area that one has not mastered and develop the ability to analyse and describe specific texts. In other words, extra demands are made on the teacher.

A further demand faced by ESP teachers comes from the fact that ESP courses often run for a limited period of time as needs and circumstances change. We saw in the scenario about Alison that the numbers of overseas-trained doctors who had immigrated to New Zealand warranted an ESP course being set up at that point of time. However, the English course for medical doctors Alison set up is unlikely to run indefinitely. Immigration patterns and government policy change and the impetus to provide such a course may end after a couple of years. In the scenario featuring Derya there had been a recent increase in the number of doctoral engineering students who needed English-language support. But this situation may not continue. In coming years, fewer doctoral students may wish to study engineering in the university. Or, if the number of prospective doctoral students continues to rise, the university may limit entry to students who already have very high levels of communicative ability in English and the ESP course may come to be seen as redundant.

1.4 Effectiveness of ESP

Given that ESP teaching makes additional demands on teachers and course developers in terms of investigating needs and designing courses that may only run for a relatively short time, it seems legitimate to ask whether teaching ESP is effective. Is there evidence to show that it is effective enough to warrant the time and energy needed to set up a course?

Empirical investigation into the effectiveness of ESP teaching has been limited (Johns and Dudley-Evans, 1991; Master, 2005). This has also been the case in EAP (Gillet and Wray, 2006). It is easy to understand why this is so. There are few situations in which an experimental study comparing a group of learners provided with an ESP-oriented course and one with similar learners provided with a general English course would be possible. There are few empirical studies investigating the effectiveness of ESP in workplace training, due in large part to issues of confidentiality in corporate culture and also time and cost constraints in ESP management (Kim, 2008, p. 16).

Master (2005, p. 109) lists a number of questions concerning the accountability of ESP including:

- Do ESP/EST (English for Science and Technology) programmes work?
- Are they more effective than previous programmes aimed at general language proficiency?
- If so, in what ways are they more effective?
- Can the expense be justified?
- Are there any unintended or unforeseen outcomes resulting from the use of any given ESP programme?

The two studies described below relate to the second of these questions posited by Master (2005): Are ESP programmes more effective than programmes aimed at general language proficiency?

Kasper (1997) conducted an experimental study to investigate the effects of academic courses linking the content of intermediate level English as a Second Language (ESL) courses to mainstream courses such as psychology in a US college setting. The study aimed to provide evidence to support the use of 'content-based' ESL instruction. In the study one group of ESL learners received ESL instruction which included a content-based reading class. In the reading class the students read selected passages from five academic disciplines, language acquisition, biology, computer science, psychology and anthropology, which were disciplines the students were most likely to study in the college. The students in the non-content-based group used a reading textbook with a range of topics (not related to specific academic disciplines). The study found that content-based instruction impacted positively on the students' academic progress and success. Kasper (1997, p. 310) explained this result saying that the students focused on gathering information/ideas from the content-based materials. The materials presented the students with complex information/ideas communicated through the second language. The students thus acquired information through sophisticated linguistic input and this helped them move to more advanced levels of language processing.

A further study in a college setting is reported in Song (2006). Like Kasper (1997), Song compared the academic performance of two groups of ESL students enrolled at the same point of time in their first semester of study. One group received one semester of content-based ESL instruction and one group received non-content-linked ESL instruction. Song tracked the progress of the two groups through their academic records. Both the content-linked and non-content-linked ESL courses aimed to help students develop academic literacy in English. However, the content-based instruction also aimed to integrate ESL study with disciplines in the college. It therefore included assignments and topics from the disciplines and provided opportunities for the learners to participate in social and academic events, such as lectures by faculty or guests. Song found that students receiving content-based instruction achieved better results in their ESL course and subsequent ESL courses as well as better long-term academic success rates than those who received non-content-based ESL instruction.

Theoretical arguments can be made as to why ESP courses should be more effective than general ESL courses. It can be argued that because ESP courses cater to students' interests and needs, they are more likely to engender high levels of motivation. It can be assumed that students will be more interested in topics and texts related to their work or study areas. If students are more motivated, then learning is more likely to occur. It can also be argued that ESP courses are more efficient because they have more limited aims than general ESL courses. Because ESP courses are based on needs analysis, the learning objectives are more highly proscribed than would be the case in general ESL courses. Thus it is not surprising that learning outcomes may be perceived more favourably. Limited and highly specified aims are more likely to be achievable.

We also need to consider how new members of disciplines, professions and vocations learn the ways of communicating in them. According to a theory developed by Lave and Wenger (1991), learning is social and involves participation in a community of practice. According to this theory when people first join a community they are on the outer borders of it and learn from the periphery. As they become increasingly competent they can move towards the centre of the community. A community of practice can be described as a group of people sharing common concerns, problems and interests and who increase their knowledge and expertise in the area by interacting with each other (Wenger, McDermot and Snyder, 2002). Wenger et al. give examples of such communities of practice – engineers who design with a particular type of electronic circuit and who find it important to get together to compare designs and soccer mums and dads who use game times to share advice about parenting. The groups may not necessarily work together or meet on a daily basis but they do interact because they find it useful to do so:

> As they (members of the group) spend time together, they typically share information, insight and advice. … They may create tools, standards, generic designs, manuals, and other documentation – or they may simply develop a tacit understanding that they share. … Over time, they develop a unique perspective on their topic as well as a body of common knowledge, practices and approaches. They also develop personal relationships and established ways of interacting. (Wenger et al., 2002, p. 5)

Communities of practice develop knowledge and act as repositories of it and are the ideal place to learn community knowledge (Wenger, 1998).

Pre-experience ESP learners cannot generally learn from within their targeted community of practice. Perhaps they feel that they do not have the language skills to work or study in the target community of practice as yet or perhaps they are excluded from it until such time as they have requisite language or communication skills in place. ESP courses offer them a middle ground between general English classes and actually being and learning in the target community. They involve the learners in the study of communication in the target community as a means for them to gain knowledge of it. This study could be in the form of reading texts produced in the community or studying patterns on interaction and language use employed in it. ESP courses can also try to offer some social links to the target community of practice. For example, in the study conducted by Song (2006), content-based instruction included contact with the target community (lectures with guest speakers and social events).

ESP courses can offer during and post-experience ESP learners time out from their work or study in their actual community of practice to work on specific aspects of ways of communicating, ways they may not have been able to acquire firmly in situ.

1.5   Summary

This chapter has shown that ESP has both variable and constant features. Its variability stems from the range of areas for which ESP courses are developed. These range from the relatively general (for example, academic English writing courses) to the highly specific (for example, English for hotel receptionists). Its variability also stems from the differing relationships ESP learners have with their target community of practice – in some cases learners are already working or studying, or have already worked or studied in their target workplaces or disciplines, and thus have knowledge of their specific ways of working. In other cases, learners may not have entered their targeted communities and have little understanding of what work or study in these communities involves. And finally, the variability in ESP stems from differences in how familiar ESP teachers are with the target disciplines, professions and vocations and their specialist discourse.

As for constants, the discussion of ESP in this chapter has shown that ESP almost invariably involves discussion of learners' needs and in viewing learners primarily in work- and study-related roles. ESP courses of necessity require a narrowing down of language and skills that are to be taught. In order to teach that language or those skills, ESP courses almost inevitably make use of texts and draw on descriptions of language use and communication from the target communities of practice and disciplines.

1.6   Discussion

1. Which areas of ESP or EAP do you currently teach or envisage teaching in the future? What background knowledge do you already have that helps or could help you in this?

1. Absolute characteristics
   - ESP is designed to meet specific needs of the learner;
   - ESP makes use of the underlying methodology and the activities of the discipline it serves;
   - ESP is centred on the language (grammar, lexis, register), skills, discourse and genres appropriate to these activities.
2. Variable characteristics
   - ESP may be related to or designed for specific disciplines;
   - ESP may use, in specific teaching situations, a different methodology from that of general English;
   - ESP is likely to be designed for adult learners, either at a tertiary level institution or in a professional work situation. It could, however, be used for learners at secondary school level;
   - ESP is generally designed for intermediate or advanced students. Most ESP courses assume basic knowledge of the language system, but it can be used with beginners.

Figure 1.3 Definition of absolute and variable characteristics of ESP
Source: Dudley-Evans and St John (1998), pp. 4–5

2. The studies by Kasper (1997) and Song (2006) offer a response to Master's (2005) question about whether ESP courses are more effective than general ESL courses. Suggest a study to address another of the questions posed by Master. What information would you collect and whom would you ask?
3. Dudley-Evans and St John (1998, pp. 4–5) offer a formal definition of ESP in Figure 1.3. This definition specifies three absolute characteristics, characteristics which are always present. It specifies four variable characteristics, characteristics which are often, but not always, present.

    Consider the ESP or EAP courses you have taught or envisage teaching in the future. Which of the 'variable characteristics' were/will be present or absent?
4. What communities of practice are you in? How did you/do you learn about the ways of communicating in them? Are you on the outside of any communities of practice that you would like to become a member of? If so, how could a language/communication class or specialist help you gain the knowledge you might need to participate in the community?
5. Do you think ESP courses should try to forge actual links between students and members of the target disciplines or communities of practice? Why or why not?

Part I
Main Considerations in ESP Course Development

2
Analysing Needs

2.1 Introduction

This chapter discusses the importance of needs analysis in ESP and describes how teachers and course developers set about investigating needs. The first section defines needs analysis. The second section presents and discusses a set of hypothetical scenarios in which ESP courses were set up without a careful investigation of needs. The third section describes the role of needs analysis in course design. The fourth section suggests ways ESP course developers and teachers can use published needs analyses to help them investigate needs in their own contexts. The final section outlines the various types of information that can be collected in a needs analysis project.

2.2 Definitions of needs analysis

ESP courses set out to teach the language and communication skills that specific groups of language learners need or will need to function effectively in their disciplines of study, professions or workplaces. Because ESP focuses on teaching specific language and communication skills, ESP course design usually includes a stage in which the course developers identify what specific language and skills the group of language learners will need. The identification of language and skills is used in determining and refining the content for the ESP course. It can also be used to assess learners and learning at the end of the course. This process is termed 'needs analysis'.

Over the years needs analysis has become increasingly sophisticated. In the early years of ESP, needs analysis tended to be construed as a fairly simple pre-course procedure involving analysis of the target situation. However, this is no longer the case (Garcia Mayo, 2000; Tajino, James and Kijima, 2005). Read the two definitions below. The first appeared in the initial volume of the journal *English for Specific Purposes* in 1980 and the second appeared in 1998.

How has the notion of needs analysis in ESP been expanded?

1. Chambers (1980):
    Needs analysis should be concerned with the establishment of communi-
    cative needs and their realisations, resulting from an analysis of the com-
    munication in the target situation – what I will refer to as target situation
    analysis.

2. Dudley-Evans and St John (1998) offer a 'current concept of needs analysis'
    (p. 125):
    A. Professional information about the learners: The tasks and activities
        learners are/will be using English for – *target situation analysis* and *objec-
        tive needs*.
    B. Personal information about the learners: Factors which may affect the
        way they learn such as previous learning experiences, cultural informa-
        tion, reasons for attending the course and expectations of it, attitude to
        English – *wants, means* and *subjective needs*.
    C. English language information about the learners: What their current
        skills and language use are – *present situation analysis* – which allows us
        to assess (D).
    D. The learners' lacks: The gap between (C) and (A) – *lacks*.
    E. Language learning information: Effective ways of learning the skills and
        language in (D) – *learning needs*.
    F. Professional communication information about (A): Knowledge of how
        language and skills are used in the target situation – *linguistic analysis,
        discourse analysis, genre analysis*.
    G. What is wanted from the course.
    H. Information about how the course will be run – *means analysis*.

West (1997, pp. 70–1) reports on the expanding concept of needs analysis and
uses the metaphor of a journey to describe the elements involved. In the early
days needs analyses focused largely on *necessities* or *objective needs* representing '*the
destination* of the learner's journey'. These analyses aimed to determine priorities,
such as, which skills (reading, writing, listening, speaking), and which situations
or tasks, such as speaking on the telephone or writing minutes from meetings,
were more or less important in the target situation. Later the concept of needs
analysis was expanded to include 'deficiency analysis' (*lacks* or the gap between
what the learner needs to know to operate in the target situation and the learner's
present language proficiency). This analysis represented *the point of departure* for
the language-learning journey. In time 'strategy analysis' (the preferred approaches
and methods in teaching and learning) was also included in needs analysis. This
represented *the means of travel*. And later 'means analysis' (identification of the
constraints and opportunities in the teaching situation) was added. This analysis
included gathering information on the classroom culture, learner factors, teacher

profiles and the status of language teaching in the organization. Means analysis represented *the ESP journey*. Amalgamating the ideas described above, the definition of needs analysis that will be used in this book is given below.

Needs analysis in ESP refers to a course development process. In this process the language and skills that the learners will use in their target professional or vocational workplace or in their study areas are identified and considered in relation to the present state of knowledge of the learners, their perceptions of their needs and the practical possibilities and constraints of the teaching context. The information obtained from this process is used in determining and refining the content and method of the ESP course. The needs analysis process involves:

- Target situation analysis: Identification of tasks, activities and skills learners are/will be using English for; what the learners should ideally know and be able to do.
- Discourse analysis: Descriptions of the language used in the above.
- Present situation analysis: Identification of what the learners do and do not know and can or cannot do in relation to the demands of the target situation.
- Learner factor analysis: Identification of learner factors such as their motivation, how they learn and their perceptions of their needs.
- Teaching context analysis: Identification of factors related to the environment in which the course will run. Consideration of what realistically the ESP course and teacher can offer.

Needs analysis should not be seen as an entirely objective procedure. Hyland (2008, p. 113) reminds us, 'Needs analysis is like any other classroom practice in that it involves decisions based on teachers' interests, values, and beliefs about teaching, learning and language.'

Sysoyev (2001) makes links between needs analysis in ESP and L. Vygotsky's (1978) notion of the Zone of Proximal Development. In this notion there are two stages in the development of an individual. The first stage represents what the learner can do independently. The second stage represents the potential of that individual and what he or she can achieve with the help of another more competent person. The Zone of Proximal Development is the distance between the two stages. The mediator is the person who helps the learners move from the first to the second stage. In ESP, the mediator is the teacher and the second stage is the realization of their needs.

2.3 Hypothetical scenarios

In this section a number of hypothetical scenarios are presented. Each shows an ESP course that set out to address language needs but despite all good intentions failed to do so in some respects. After reading each scenario, consider what went wrong and suggest reasons why the ESP course failed to meet expectations.

2.3.1 The English for general academic purposes discussion skills course

The Department of English Language Studies in a university decides to offer a discussion skills course to complement the existing English for General Academic Purposes programme for undergraduate students. The programme currently has courses on academic writing and listening. Students on the programme have mentioned that they are struggling to communicate orally and participate in their subject classes. The teachers in the English Language Unit meet to discuss what the content of the discussion skills course should be. They recall their own student days. Most of them had studied arts subjects such as history, foreign languages and literature and could remember the heated seminar discussions they participated in and the lively discussions they had enjoyed. They decide to develop the discussion skills course around a set of general interest topics and issues, such as whether the government should continue to fund student fees. When the teachers tell the students in their writing and listening classes about the discussion skills course that will soon be offered, the students appear enthusiastic.

The next year the course and materials are ready. In the first semester relatively few students enrol for the course and most of those who do already have very good speaking skills. In the second semester even fewer students enrol and these seem to have even better speaking skills.

- What seems to have gone wrong?
- What was missing from the investigation of needs?

2.3.1.1 *Analysis*

It is clear that the type of students the course had aimed to attract have in fact not been attracted to this course. In fact, the course appears to be attracting students who already have good speaking and discussion skills. What has gone wrong in terms of needs analysis here? The teachers/course developers did not find out how important academic speaking events actually are in the target situation. Students nearly always need to write assignments and answer examination questions and attend some form of lectures (and this explains why they are attracted to the courses offered on academic writing and listening). However, for many students, speaking events are relatively infrequent in their academic studies. The teachers did not investigate how important speaking is. The teachers had mainly studied art subjects themselves. Such subjects often include more discussion and seminars than other disciplines such as the hard sciences. Needs may vary considerably in different disciplines. Was this considered? The teachers reflected on the modes of instruction they had experienced as university students. But what may have been true in the past may no longer be so.

The teachers/course developers also needed to find out students' perceptions about the importance of academic speaking (learner factor analysis). For example, are the students assessed on their participation in discussions and seminars? In which disciplines and subjects are the students required to make presentations and how important are the grades they receive for them? If a skill or aspect of language use is not particularly important, it is unlikely that students will be motivated to invest valuable time in it.

The teachers/course developers neglected to investigate how often the students participate in class discussion in their subject classes and the students' perceptions of how important discussion skills are. Questions such as those below could have been used to survey the students:

1. Do you need to participate in class discussions as part of your university studies?
   Yes/No

   If yes,

   How frequent are class discussions?

   How are you assessed (if at all) on this?

2. Are you required to give presentations?
   Yes/No

   If yes,

   How frequent are these presentations?

   How are you assessed (if at all) on these?

3. Rank the following skills in terms of their importance for your academic studies:

   Writing
   Speaking
   Listening
   Reading

4. How important on a scale of 0–5 are the following for success in your studies? 5 is very important and 0 is not important at all.

   Academic writing
   Academic speaking
   Academic listening
   Academic reading

Had the teachers/course developers found that speaking does feature quite strongly for the students and is important for them, they could have investigated needs in more detail by observing speak events in the university (target situation analysis) and learners' ability to speak in academic events (present situation analysis).

2.3.2   The writing course for overseas-trained dentists

A number of overseas-trained dentists have immigrated to an English-speaking country. They are preparing to sit the registration exams which, if they pass, will allow them to work as dentists. A government-sponsored bridging programme has been established to help them prepare for the exams. The course is run at a university. The programme provides courses on medical and dental topics, ethical issues and the law surrounding medical practices in the country.

The English-language-teaching unit at the university has been approached by the organizers of the bridging programme and asked to provide an English writing course. It has been noted that the writing of some of the overseas-trained dentists who sat the registration exams to date was poorly organized and expressed. The English-language unit appoints a teacher. The teacher, who is given very little time to develop the course, devises a syllabus focusing on paragraph and essay organization and based on topics related to dentistry, such as, the addition of fluoride to tap water and the relationship between smoking and diseases of the mouth (topics that the teacher has discovered from reading recent issues of the regional dental journal).

In teaching the course, the teacher devotes a good deal of time to responding to the students' writing. She provides feedback and corrections on the students' writing in terms of organization and breakdowns in meaning. Often she reformulates the students' sentences.

Half way through the course the teacher conducts a course evaluation. The class members are very positive about the efforts of the teacher on their behalf and they have clearly appreciated the very detailed feedback on their writing the teacher has supplied. The teacher is surprised to find that although they feel the writing course has been useful for developing their ability to write in English generally, they think it will have limited impact on their actual performance in the registration exams and would prefer to spend the remaining time before the exams preparing by self-study rather than continuing with the writing classes.

- What seems to have gone wrong?
- What was missing from the investigation of needs?

2.3.2.1   *Analysis*

The class members are voting with their feet. They feel the course does not meet their needs and would prefer to spend their time in self-study. Why did the teacher set up and run a course with limited relevance to needs? The teacher has relied exclusively on one source of information about the students' needs – the bridging course organizers. The organizers are not language teachers and most probably have a limited understanding of the nature of language use and communication and only a partial understanding of the nature of writing and written text. The bridging course organizers have requested a course in 'written English' and the teacher has provided one without conducting her own investigation and analysis of needs. She has not investigated the students' perceptions of their needs (learner factors analysis). In assessing needs it can be important to consider more than one party's view of needs.

What the teacher could have done was make her own assessment of the tasks the students would be using English for. In this case, the overseas-trained dentists are focused entirely on passing their registration exam. They are less interested in developing their general ability to write English even on topics related to dentistry. We would expect that the dentists want to know what writing tasks or genres they are expected to write on in the exam and that they would like to have these genres described and deconstructed for them so that they can master them. There is also a clash here between the bridging course organizers' focus on long-term needs – to develop the dentists' ability to write in English – and the short-term needs, as seen by the dentist themselves, to know enough about what text types they will be required to write in the exam. The teacher needs also to make a teaching-context analysis and ask what can realistically be achieved by the ESP course. In this case, the course is short term and so realistically cannot do much to develop writing proficiency per se.

The teacher could have talked to the overseas-trained dentists as well as the bridging course organisers before she developed the course and materials. She could have examined past copies of the registration exam and analysed the writing tasks and the discourse and genre features they entailed (discourse and genre analysis).

Some questions to guide the teacher's investigation of needs can be suggested:

1. How do the different parties (the bridging course organizers and the overseas dentists) describe needs?
2. What kinds of writing (text types) are involved in the exam and what difficulties do the students have with them?
3. What realistically can be taught about writing these texts types in a limited time period?

The teacher could also interview the dentists to find out about their learning styles. It is possible that as mature and highly educated adults they would prefer self-study options and some one-on-one or small group sessions to get feedback on their writing rather than through a whole class, teacher-fronted option.

2.3.3   The language for care home workers course

Anna has been asked to provide language support for a small group of care home workers. They have come from an East Asian country to work in a rest home and hospital facility for the elderly in an English-speaking country. Most of the care workers were formerly nurses in their home countries. Their role as care workers involves looking after the physical and emotional needs of the elderly residents. The facility's nursing and medical staff members are pleased with the work the new care workers do. However, there have been some complaints from the residents about difficulties communicating with the new group of care workers. The nursing manager reports that when she questioned the residents about the problem they mentioned poor pronunciation and not being able to understand the care workers' accents.

Anna, a relative of one of the facility's medical officers, has just finished a MA programme in English Language Teaching and before that she taught English in a small language school in Thailand for a year. On the MA programme she took courses in a range of subjects such as second-language acquisition, descriptions of modern English language and language testing. There was no ESP course on offer. Anna is employed by the rest care facility to provide a weekly two-hour session to help the care workers improve their pronunciation and speaking. Anna works with the care workers to help achieve clear enunciation. She finds out from the care workers which language expressions, conversational routines and vocabulary they use regularly with the residents. Anna uses role plays in her teaching and encourages the care workers to use 'clear enunciation' in them. She introduces them to a number of self-study techniques for working on pronunciation and speaking.

Anna is surprised to find that even in her first teaching session with the care workers she had almost no difficulty understanding the care workers' accents or pronunciation herself. The language sessions prove to be a lot of fun and the care workers take their self-studies seriously. The care workers enjoy their time out from caring for the elderly residents. Everyone is happy, except that is for the residents who continue to complain.

- What seems to have gone wrong?
- What was missing from the investigation of needs?

2.3.3.1   *Analysis*

The course that Anna has offered has appealed to the care workers but has clearly not met the needs for which it was set up as the patients do not feel communication has improved. As in the previous scenario, the initial analysis of the problem has been made by a non-language specialist (the nursing manager) who simply took the patients' assessment of the problem at face value.

The question remains – what perceived needs of the patients are the care workers failing to meet? If Anna can follow the care workers' pronunciation, then it is unlikely that pronunciation is the cause of the problem here. There is a communication problem but it has been wrongly identified.

Anna needs to conduct her own investigation to try to identify the source of the problem. She could observe the patients interacting with the care workers and try to identify for herself the root cause of communication difficulties rather than relying on second-hand reports. Possible causes of the problem include the care workers' speaking too softly or not using enough repetition and confirmation checks. Anna could usefully compare interactions between patients and the established care workers in the facility and between them and the cohort of new care workers. What is it the new cohort does differently in terms of communication and interaction? Is it possible that the established care workers give fuller explanations to the patients about what is going on or what they need to do? Is it possible that more experienced care workers use less technical medical terms or less formal language? Is it possible that they use more humour in their interactions? Is there really a problem here at all? Is it a language problem? Is it a problem related to some or all of the new care workers? Is it a problem of unrealistic expectations on the part of the residents? She could observe how the experienced care workers and the new cohort of care workers interact with the patients. These are the kind of areas Anna could investigate.

2.4   Needs analysis as a course design process

The above scenarios show how important it is to explore and consider needs before setting up a course of instruction. It the first scenario, a more considered analysis of needs and the situation may have deterred the teachers from setting up an academic discussion skills course. In the second case, the information gleaned from needs analysis could have helped the teacher focus instruction on key written genres important for the registration exam. The focus of the course may then have been sufficiently narrowed down to appeal to the class. In the third case, findings from observations may have led to the development of a course with a very different focus such as interaction skills.

Needs analysis also plays a role in refining and evaluating ongoing ESP courses. For example, in the second scenario, in coming years the dental registration exam may change and different types of writing may be required. Clearly, the ESP teacher will need this information to revise her course. Or, the teacher becomes increasing familiar with the medical staff on the bridging course and this allows her to examine past exam papers to see what strengths and weaknesses are evident in candidates' writing. She may be able to interview those who mark the exams to find out what they see as strengths and weaknesses in sample papers. She could then include a focus on these precise areas in her teaching.

Pre-course needs analysis   →   Initial course design

Ongoing needs analysis   →   Revision of course design

Figure 2.1   The role of needs analysis in course design

Teachers working on ESP courses often find that their understanding of the target situation or learners' needs develop as they work on the ESP course and that they use this developing understanding to modify the course. If the teachers work within the target situation such as the teacher on the bridging course, they are often able to gain increased access over time to information such as the end users' perspectives. All of this provides valuable information that can be used to refine the existing ESP course.

In its simplest form, needs analysis is a pre-course design process in which information is gathered to help the teacher or course developer decide what the course should focus on, what content in terms of language or skills to include and what teaching/learning methods to employ. Over time needs can change and teachers also gain increased understanding of the situation and the learners' needs in relation to it. Thus needs analysis also plays a role in refining the ESP course once it is set up and running. See Figure 2.1.

2.5   Building on existing knowledge

It has been suggested in the previous sections of this chapter that teachers or course developers need to carefully investigate needs when setting up or refining ESP courses. The examples given so far about how to investigate needs have all been suggestions for collecting primary data, that is, suggestions for analysing needs from scratch. However, sometimes other ESP courses have been set up for similar situations or students and reports on these have been published. The teacher or course developer can glean useful information or ideas from these reports to help in his or her own needs analysis project. The teacher or course developer can use the reports on these established courses as a starting point for conceptualizing needs and getting ideas about what kind of data to collect and how to gather it. In other words, not all the thinking and information gathering needs to be done ab initio.

2.5.1   The English for general academic purposes discussion skills course

It would have been possible to delve into some of the research literature in the initial stages of considering whether to establish the course. A number of studies have aimed to identify the skills university students need. The studies investigated needs in other contexts and so the actual findings have only limited relevance. However, the studies often raise a number of issues that could have been a useful point of departure for the teachers in our scenario.

Two published studies focusing on identification of students' listening and speaking needs that could have helped in this scenario are *Students' Views of Academic Aural/Oral Skill: A Comparative Analysis* by D. Ferris (1998) and *Academic Oral Communication Needs of East Asian International Graduate Students in Non-Science and Non-Engineering Fields* by S. Kim (2006).

Ferris (1998) surveyed over 700 ESL students and 200 faculty members at three tertiary institutions in the US. In one part of the survey, students were asked about the aural/oral skills needed in their studies. The study revealed that the two speaking skills most students required 'always' or 'often' were class participation and small group work and the skills required only 'sometimes' or 'never' were class debates, student-led discussions and formal speeches (p. 299). Interestingly, the speaking skills the students reported as 'always' or 'often' finding difficult were those they least required (formal speeches, discussion leading and class debate).

The survey showed that the skills needed varied according to institution, course level, class size and academic discipline. It also showed that student and faculty responses differed considerably. In explaining these differences, Ferris points out that professors 'may not always be the best judges of the ways in which their students are struggling ... by the same token, students may not be the most accurate informants on what the professors actually require' (p. 307).

Kim (2006) investigated the needs of East Asian graduate students at a US university using a web-based questionnaire to survey 280 students. The questionnaire asked about their listening/speaking skill requirements, their perceptions of their difficulties in meeting these requirements and which particular listening or speaking skills they saw as important for their academic success.

Some results from Kim's (2006) study contrasted with the results of Ferris' (1998) study. Kim found, for example, that the great majority of students reported they always or frequently were expected to participate in whole-class discussions, discuss readings or participate in small group discussion activities in class. Some findings were similar: raising questions in class was a common requirement. The respondents in Kim's study found leading class discussions the most difficult listening/speaking skill, followed by participating in whole-class discussions, then participating in small group discussions and next giving formal oral academic presentations. The survey asked the respondents to rank the degree of importance of the skill areas including pronunciation, understanding lectures, general listening comprehension, note-taking skills, oral presentations and class participation. Students ranked oral presentations as the most important and pronunciation as the least important.

Kim discusses some of the discrepancies between the findings of her study showing the emphasis the students put on small group discussion compared to that of Ferris saying:

> While the current study identified small group discussions as one of the most frequently required oral classroom tasks, following whole class discussions, Ferris reported that students were rarely asked to participate in small group activities. These findings may indicate that graduate-level classes tend to be smaller than undergraduate classes, so it is easier for graduate course instructors to set up discussion in small groups followed by group reports to the whole class. It may also come from instructors' changing instructional preferences. (p. 6)

These two studies offer a number of issues and ideas for needs analysis.

1. The studies show that graduate and undergraduate speaking/discussion needs can vary. The teachers in our scenario fondly recalled the lively discussion they had participated in during their studies but did these take place during their undergraduate or graduate level studies? Memories are not the best source of data. And, as Kim (2006) argues, instructors' preferences change.
2. The report of Ferris' study includes the survey used. The teachers in the scenario could use the questions and format involved as a source of ideas to help them develop a questionnaire or set of interview prompts for use in their own context.
3. Both the study by Ferris and the study by Kim centred on three issues: what skills were needed, which were perceived as more or less difficult by the students and which were perceived as more or less critical for academic success. This conceptualization could be of help to the teachers in our scenario. For example, an EAP course could be devised to address the specific skills needed but if the students do not perceive themselves to have difficulty with these skills the course is unlikely to be well received.
4. Ferris' study showed that professor's and students' perceptions of requirements and difficulties diverged somewhat. The implication for needs analysis is that ideas on needs may need to be gathered from the different parties concerned.

2.5.2   The language for care home workers course

In considering needs for the care home workers course, Anna could have usefully consulted some of the literature on language needs of care workers or nurses in similar situations. One study offering useful perspectives in this area is 'From

Needs Analysis to Curriculum Development: Designing a Course in Health-Care Communication for Immigrant Students in the USA' by Susan Bolsher and Kari Smalkoski, published in *English for Specific Purposes* in 2002. Bolsher and Smalkoski's study investigated the needs of immigrant nursing students, many of whom were enrolled in ESL programmes in a college setting in the US. The needs analysis comprised a number of sources of information (ESL nursing students, ESL programme director and nursing faculty members) and different types of information including interviews, observations and questionnaires. The needs analysis revealed that the main area of difficulty for the students was communicating with clients and colleagues in clinical settings. The faculty reported that the nursing students sometimes had difficulty understanding the clients (the patients). An example of such a difficulty is reported below:

> I'm not sure if Mary [a pseudonym] just doesn't understand clients because she is an ESL student or if she doesn't comprehend what the clients are saying, or both. Just last week one of her elderly clients in the orthopaedic rotation was asking her questions about medication. Instead of asking the client for clarification she acted like she understood what the client was saying. ... We teach students that certain clients will be more difficult to understand or even comprehend. It's not just ESL students who are having trouble with this. (p. 62)

Other difficulties pointed out by faculty included students not being comprehended because of inappropriate stress and intonation and their low volume of speech. Observations of the students' performance in interactions revealed additional problems such as the immigrant nursing students' lack of assertiveness with clients and their avoidance of eye contact with the clients. Additional findings brought to light included difficulty with rate of speech, especially with elderly clients; understanding clients, particularly those who spoke non-standard dialects of English; making small talk with and understanding when clients were making small talk with them; and understanding how cultural values may impact on interaction with clients.

This report could have been of help to Anna in the following ways:

1. Firstly, the report identified a range of communication difficulties. This could have provided food for thought for Anna in trying to work out needs in her own situation. The analysis of Bosher and Smalkoski showed that communication problems could not be attributed to a single factor such as the immigrant nurses' pronunciation but to a number of factors.
2. Secondly, it provides a useful list of potential difficulties in a somewhat comparable situation. Anna could have used this list as a point of departure for her own investigation of needs in the rest care facility.

3. Thirdly, the report offers an example of use of multiple methods in needs analysis. Anna might have considered using a variety of methods in investigating needs in the rest home.

4. Finally, the appendix to the report provides the questionnaire used to elicit the nursing students' perspectives of their difficulties in health care communication. Possibly, Anna could have used or adapted this survey for use in her own situation.

2.6   Types of information to collect

In needs analysis the quality of the data collected depends in large part on selecting appropriate data collection techniques. Unless the course developers or teachers conducting the needs analysis have large quantities of time to devote to the project, they will need to be selective about what type of data to collect. Needs analysis can take a number of forms including questionnaires, interviews, observations of interactions and analysis of language use in the target situation, tests of performance and observations of ESP learners carrying out tasks replicating those in the target situation. Figure 2.2 shows the questionnaire Bacha and Bahous (2008) developed for an investigation into the English-language needs of business students at the Lebanese American University. Item 1 in the questionnaire inquires into the students' perceptions of the relative importance of different language skills. Item 2 inquires into how they perceive their abilities in the various skills. The remaining items focus on the writing skill in particular.

Student questionnaire

(A parallel questionnaire was used for the Faculty as it relates to their students)

Dear Student: Fill out this questionnaire as accurately as you can by circling the appropriate number according to the following scale with 4 being the most.

Please do not write your name. The purpose of this questionnaire is to find your opinions of your writing in the major.

Major: _____

1. Rank choices 1–4 which skill is most important to your major.

    a. Reading   4 3 2 1
    b. Writing   4 3 2 1
    c. Speaking 4 3 2 1
    d. Listening 4 3 2 1

2. Circle the number that best indicates your perception of your language ability in the major.

    a. Listening 4 3 2 1
    b. Speaking 4 3 2 1
    c. Reading   4 3 2 1
    d. Writing   4 3 2 1

Figure 2.2   An example questionnaire used in needs analysis
Source: Bacha and Bahous (2008), pp. 89–90

3. Circle the number that best indicates your writing ability of the below in the major.

    a. Sentence structure and vocabulary 4 3 2 1
    b. Ideas 4 3 2 1
    c. Organization of ideas 4 3 2 1

4. What kind of writing do you do in the major ☐ (4 a lot, 3 sometimes, 2 rarely, 1 never)

    a. Essay assignments   4 3 2 1
    b. Essay tests   4 3 2 1
    c. Letters   4 3 2 1
    d. Lab and reports   4 3 2 1
    e. Research papers   4 3 2 1
    f. Summary of lectures 4 3 2 1
    g. Note-taking in class 4 3 2 1
    h. Note-taking/internet 4 3 2 1
    i. Other: Specify _____ 4 3 2 1

5. To what extent do you improve in the writing needed for the major over the semester ☐

    a. A great deal
    b. A sufficient amount to deal with the course work
    c. Not enough
    d. None at all
    e. Already have a satisfactory level

6. The teaching of writing should be the responsibility of (check all that apply).

    a. The English teacher
    b. The content-area teacher in the major
    c. Both the English and content-area teacher in the major
    Other: specify _____

Faculty interview questions

Do your students have language problems? ☐
Do you use languages other than English in the class to explain the material? ☐
What types of language problems do they have? ☐
How do you deal with these problems? ☐
Do you find that students improve by the end of the semester? ☐
Do you think they are improving due to English? ☐

Figure 2.2 Continued

    Most needs analyses include the use of either questionnaires or interviews. Works on research methodology often include discussions on how to construct and administer a questionnaire or interview. See, for example, Kumar (1996), Mackey and Gass (2005) and Nunan (1992). It is not uncommon for needs analysis projects to include both questionnaires and interviews, often interviewing a subset of respondents who completed a questionnaire, or developing a set of questionnaire items from information collected in interviews.

    Kumar (1996) discusses the advantages and drawbacks of questionnaires and interviews. Questionnaires do not take long to administer and it is often possible to get information from a large number of respondents. The responses are anonymous and thus respondents will hopefully offer their opinions and ideas frankly. Interviews are time consuming and because of this the investigator can often only interview a few people. However, in an interview the investigator can probe responses and thus gain an in-depth understanding of the opinions and information offered. Additionally, unclear questions or answers can be clarified during an interview.

Both types of data collection potentially have drawbacks. For example, people tend to think carefully about questionnaire items before responding. This may lead respondents to try to provide idealized responses (responses they see as socially desirable). Good interviewing skills do not come naturally to everyone and some interviewers may let their own opinions come across too strongly and lead to bias in the interview. See Figure 2.3.

Questionnaires and interviews allow the needs analyst to explore people's opinions of needs, difficulties and the importance of language skills and areas. However, needs analysts also investigate actual samples of language use or learners' performance in events in the target situation. Direct means can be used to investigate these areas. To investigate language use in the target environment, examples of the types of texts used in them can be collected and analysed. For example, if the care workers in Anna's rest home facility were required as part of their work to write reports on their clients and were understood to have difficulties with this, Anna could collect samples of the reports written by a number

Questionnaires	
Advantages	Disadvantages
Less time and energy consuming to administer	Self-selecting bias. Not everyone who receives the questionnaire returns it and those who do may have different attitudes than those who do not
Offer greater anonymity to respondents	Lack of opportunity to clarify issues
	Do not allow for spontaneous responses
	Respondents may consult with one another before answering
Interviews	
Advantages	Disadvantages
More useful for collecting in-depth information	More time consuming
Opportunity for questions to be explained and responses clarified	Quality of the data obtained depends on the skills of the interviewer
	The interviewer may introduce his or her bias
	Less standardized. For example, the quality of the data may vary when different interviewers are used.

Figure 2.3   Advantages and disadvantages of questionnaires and interviews
Source: Based on discussion in Kumar (1996)

of different care workers and could adopt a genre-based approach to analysis by identifying the kind of information the reports typically include, how it is organized sequentially and any features of language use associated with it. This topic will be examined in Chapter 3. To investigate learners' performance in events in the target situation, learners can be observed while performing tasks in the target situation (or tasks replicating events from the target situation can be used in a classroom situation). For example, if the care workers in Anna's rest home facility are understood to have difficulties making small talk with clients, Anna could observe some of the workers engaged in episodes of small talk with the clients (and possibly compare their performance with that of workers seen as having good language/communication skills in this area). Anna could develop a protocol to structure her observations. Possible items for inclusion in the observation protocol are:

When and where does small talk take place?
How is it initiated? (Note some samples of language use.)
What topics are included?
What kinds of questions do the care workers or clients use? (Note samples of language use.)
What kinds of responses do the care workers or clients provide? (Note samples of language use.)
Are any difficulties apparent? (If so, what are they?)
What appears to keep the episodes going or to lead to an abrupt end?
How long do the episodes generally last?
How are episodes closed down? (Note examples of actual language use.)

Questionnaires, interviews and observations are often the main data sources used in needs analysis. However, sometimes additional information enhances the needs analysis project. Ethnographic methods were used to collect information in an investigation of academic writing needs by Molle and Prior (2008). These methods included in-depth interviews with faculty and students, genre analysis of students' texts, class observations and collection of course materials such as syllabuses and handouts (p. 545). Types of information in needs analysis listed in Johns and Price-Machada (2001) include interviews with experts (for example, with supervisors in the target situation in which the learners will work) as well as the workers or learners themselves, job-shadowing (the everyday language experiences of workers in a typical day at work), analysis of the learning style of the learners, analysis of modes of working (for example, team work or individual work) and spoken or written reflections (for example, learners could be asked to reflect on what they have experienced on an ESP programme as a basis for planning a new programme or revising the current programme).

2.7 Summary

As shown in this chapter, needs analysis is a key component in ESP course design and development. Johns and Price-Machada (2001, p. 49) argue that it is an obligatory step: 'In every genuine ESP course, needs assessment is obligatory, and in many programs, an ongoing needs assessment is integral to curriculum design and evaluation.' Over the years, needs analysis has become increasingly sophisticated and has come to encompass not only analysis of language use and skills in the target situation but analysis of learner factors and teaching context factors as well.

Various types of information can be collected in a needs analysis and ESP teachers and course developers decide what type of information to collect on a case-by-case basis. If they wish to investigate learners' difficulties in speaking, they might decide to observe the learners' performance in speaking situations. If they wish to investigate writing needs and difficulties, they may collect samples of their learners' writing and writing tasks from the target situation. If they wish to investigate the comprehension needs of their learners they are likely to use either questionnaire or interview items to elicit the learners' perceptions of difficulties as comprehension difficulties cannot generally be directly observed.

It has been argued in the chapter that one useful point of departure for a needs analysis project is to locate published reports of ESP-oriented needs analyses in roughly comparable situations. These reports often provide examples of how others have conceptualized the area or set about identifying needs in it.

2.8   Discussion

1. Suggest reasons why you might use both a questionnaire and an interview in a needs analysis project.
2. Select an article that reports a needs analysis, or an article that reports a course design but includes an account of the needs assessment on which the course was based. Possible sources of such published reports are *English for Specific Purposes*, the *Journal of English for Academic Purposes*, or journals published locally. Present a summary of what the needs analysis involved (target situation analysis, deficiency analysis, learner factor analysis, and so on), the procedure followed and the types of data collected.
3. Describe an ESP teaching situation you could conceivably face in the future. Which experts might you wish to interview in order to gain insights into the demands your learners face or will face in the target situation? Develop a set of interview prompts you could use to interview one of these experts.
4. The teachers who developed the academic discussion skills course in the first scenario did not observe subject classes in the university to determine what

types of academic discussion (if any) occur and the features of any such discussions. Develop an observation protocol that they could use.

5. You have been assigned to develop and teach an ESP course for bank tellers who will shortly be transferred to the foreign exchange sections of their banks in a country in the Middle East. Outline the steps you would take to investigate their English language needs.

3
Investigating Specialist Discourse

Chapter 2 focused on a key procedure in ESP course development, needs analysis. However, needs analysis itself does not provide information on specialist discourse and before teachers and course developers start planning the curriculum, they often need to obtain descriptions of discourse (communication and language use) identified in the needs analysis. This leads to the topic of the present chapter, investigations of specialist discourse.

ESP curricula generally focus strongly on the description and illustration of communication and language use in the specialist field. Thus the language content of ESP courses is pivotal in ESP course design. Many courses are strongly focused on language content (as opposed to content of another nature, such as learning strategies). Many courses have as a major objective that the students will have better understanding of communication and language use in the specialist field or target discourse community by the end of the course. Moreover, such courses generally aim to offer realistic descriptions of discourse derived from empirical investigations of communication and language use in the community or specialist field.

This chapter considers the importance of descriptions of specialist discourse in ESP. It discusses the circumstances in which teachers and course developers conduct their own investigations, and describes ways to do this. To this end, three approaches to the investigation of specialist discourse, ethnography, genre analysis and corpus analysis are introduced.

3.1   Importance of descriptions of specialist discourse in ESP

ESP endeavours to teach the language the learners need to communicate effectively in their work or study areas. Given this central premise, it goes without saying that the language content of the course needs to be based on detailed, accurate and realistic descriptions of how language is actually used in these areas. To illustrate – if a teacher is developing a course that will focus on written communication for nurses, materials and content in the course will need to be based on the writing situations the nurses are expected to face either currently or in future. The teacher or course developer will need to understand the writing situations and the types of the discourse they involve, for example, the texts the nurses are or will be required to write, and features of language use in them.

Let us turn to an example of an investigation of specialist discourse. Parks (2001) investigated the written communication of nurses in two specific settings and focused on one important type of text (genre) that the nurses produced, the nursing care plan. One finding this study brought to light was that the nurses (especially student nurses) were expected to use nursing rather than medical terms. For example, one of the participants in Parks' study reported having used the nursing term 'burning when voiding' rather than the medical term 'urinary tract infection' (p. 416).

Although the impetus for Parks' study was not ESP course development, findings and descriptions of discourse in the study could be of interest to teachers and course developers designing an ESP course for nurses or nursing students. Firstly, the study identifies a key genre, the nursing care plan, and offers insights into the role this genre plays in a specific nursing community. Secondly, it provides information on features of the nursing care plan and offers insights into why these features are present. The functions and features of this genre may vary somewhat according to different nursing settings. Nevertheless ESP teachers and course developers would find this study a useful reference. They may consider, for example, if the nursing care plan is a key written genre in the target settings of the nurses or prospective nurses in their ESP class and if expectations for the forms and features of the nursing care plan described in Parks' study are similar to those in these settings. The study can provide the ESP teacher and course designer with food for thought in terms of language content for an ESP course. Could 'nursing care plans' constitute a module of the ESP course? Could distinctions between nursing and medical terms constitute a focus in the course's vocabulary syllabus?

The above example has illustrated two ways an investigation of specialist discourse can feed into ESP course development. One way was by providing concepts about communication and language use in a community of practice that teachers and course developers could use in their own investigations. The other way was by providing descriptions of language use that might feed directly into teachers' and course developers' decision making about the language content of the course.

One debate in ESP concerns the question of specificity or how specific ESP courses need to be. Writers such as Hyland (2002, 2006) advocate highly specific options arguing that the features of a text are influenced by the community in which it was produced and thus these features can be best understood and taught in relation to those communities (2006, p. 41). This debate will be described in

Chapter 4 since it impinges most directly on course design. However, at this point, I would like to examine two scripts involving questioning in specific settings. The aim is to show how the features of questioning are distinctive to those settings. As the reader will see, features of discourse illustrated in the excerpts bear limited correspondence to question-answer sequences in everyday conversational English.

Excerpt 1 is from a university tutorial on a Business Administration programme. It shows the interaction between a small group of students and the lecturer leading the tutorial. The lecturer is asking the students about their responses to questions they have prepared in advance of the class.

Excerpt 1

LECTURER: Right, so what is the first question? Value added I think. It might be a good idea if we go around the class people. Going around might get the chance to answer the questions and then we can sort of wind the discussion around some of these questions depending on the time we have.

STUDENT 1: The value added is the total value we have minus the materials and services cost.

LECTURER: Right, it's simply the (Student 1: Turnover) * the sales revenue or turnover of cost supported by materials and services. And how about then the notion of gross domestic product at market prices – would you (gesturing) like to?

STUDENT 2: Is it the value of all the goods and services produced for the domestic // market?

LECTURER: // Right domestic that's right yes.

STUDENT 3: ** So it's consumers' expenditure and government consumption?

LECTURER: Yes, that is the expenditure basis. *You might say that in a question of that sort you are actually being asked to produce some kind of link between 'value added' and 'Gross National Product' (GDP). The notion of value added can be linked in this way, say one way of measuring output, and I think you're right to bring out the expenditure categories because in fact the GDP in market prices would initially be actually estimated on the expenditure basis rather than the output basis.

STUDENT 1: ** That's including taxes and subsidies and things like that?

LECTURER: That's right yes * because ...

( ) a turn from a speaker during another speaker's turn
// marks the beginning of an overlapping turn

Basturkmen (1995, pp. 55–6)

Some of the features of this discourse are immediately apparent. The discourse is lecturer-led and shows a typical elicitation sequence of teacher/lecturer initiation, student's response and a (optional) feedback move by the teacher/lecturer, a sequence widely reported in the literature on educational discourse (Adger, 2001; Johnstone, 2008). Other features include lecturer feedback moves to expand on information the students provide and to reformulate and clearly articulate the students' prior responses (shown in the segments beginning *), and the use of clarification requests by the students to check their understanding (shown in segments beginning **).

How then might the EAP teacher draw on this excerpt to illustrate academic spoken discourse? Firstly, the teacher could use it to illustrate the functions of talk in lecturer-led discussion. The teacher might, for example, point out the importance of the feedback move as a way lecturers use to offer a clear articulation of a theme or to provide additional information on it. Secondly, the teacher might use the excerpt to illustrate features of language use, such as, students' use of statements beginning with 'So' and having a question-like intonation to introduce and preface clarification requests (for example, *So it's consumers' expenditure and government consumption?*).

We have looked at ways that even a very short segment from a text produced in the target situation could be of value to EAP teachers. However, the excerpt and description of discourse shown above would be of limited interest to teachers in a different branch of ESP, such as English for medical doctors or police officers. The practices of questioning in medical encounters (see Ainsworth-Vaughn, 2001 for a review) and police communities have their own discourse features reflecting functions and values related to work in these communities. Excerpt 2 is taken from an article by Gibbons (2001). Gibbons investigated questioning and the issuing of cautions in police interviews in New South Wales, Australia.

Excerpt 2

POLICE OFFICER: You are not obliged to say anything or do anything unless you wish to do so, but whatever you say or do will be electronically recorded and may be used in evidence. Do you understand that?
SUSPECT: Yeah.
POLICE OFFICER: Do you agree that prior to the commencement of this interview I told you that I intended asking you further questions about this matter?
SUSPECT: Yeah but =x=
POLICE OFFICER: =x= Well, do you agree that =y=
SUSPECT: =y= I don't want to say nothing.
POLICE OFFICER: OK
SUSPECT: Cause I can't remember.
POLICE OFFICER: That's all right, but do you agree that prior, before I commenced this interview, in the presence of Mr Kennett, I told you that I was going to ask you some questions about =x=
SUSPECT: =x= Yeah. Yeah. Yeah.

Gibbons, 2001, p. 452

Similar to the first excerpt, one party, the police officer, is leading the interaction by initiating the exchanges and topics (in Excerpt 1, the lecturer led the interaction). Furthermore, like the first excerpt, the second party (the suspect) appears to have been forewarned about this questioning (in Excerpt 1, the lecturer set questions prior to the tutorial). Beyond this, however, a number of differences are apparent in the function of questioning in this excerpt. Gibbons explains that 'for reasons of both effectiveness and social justice, police need to be careful in their handling of the core questioning part of the interview, in order to be fair to the interviewee, to obtain the maximum quantity of useful information, and to ensure that the interview is admissible as evidence in court' (p. 445). We see in this excerpt that the police officer is keen to establish very clearly that the suspect understands the implications of his or her responses for any ensuing court case and that he or she does not interrupt the suspect.

The excerpts have illustrated ways the 'simple' act of questioning can be enacted in academic and police work settings. Different professions and disciplines have their own specific ways of communicating and we saw in two short transcripts, one from an academic tutorial and one from a police interview, some distinctive features of types of questioning in these two fields.

3.2   When teachers/course developers conduct investigations

Although many ESP teachers and course developers might like to conduct their own empirical research (research involving collecting and analysing primary data) into specialist discourse, they only sometimes have sufficient time or means to do so. The discussion of functions and features in Excerpt 1 (the university tutorial) could lead an EAP teacher or course developer to make his or her own investigation of specific purpose language and communication. The teacher or course developer might, for instance, attend tutorials in his or her local context with the aim of developing the description or comparing the practices portrayed in it to ones occurring locally. Section 3.3 offers practical information to teachers and course developers about how to go about conducting such research. However, investigating discourse is generally a time-consuming endeavour. Even attending a relatively limited number of tutorials might require more time than many EAP teachers and course developers have. Before launching into empirical research, teachers and course developers should consider if this kind of research is necessary. In other words, when do ESP teachers and course developers need to conduct their own empirical investigations by observing events and/or collecting samples of discourse? Which circumstances would demand this? The following scenarios describe two ESP situations, one situation in which I believe an empirical investigation of specialist communication and discourse was called for and one in which it was not.

Scenario 1

My own introduction to ESP course development provides an example of a situation that in hindsight I realize called for empirical investigation of specialist discourse. A number of years ago some colleagues and I were asked to devise an English language class to support students in their first year of undergraduate study in Arts and Design Faculty. They were studying Arts – a range of subjects including Interior Design, Fine Arts and Graphic Design. In those relatively early years of ESP, descriptions of discourse and communication in specific fields were few and far between and my colleagues and I were not aware of any published research into discourse in Fine Arts and design fields. Nor were we aware of any published ESP course books for this target audience.

We did some preliminary needs analysis to find out about the target situation (the courses the students would be studying, the assignments and the speaking and writing situations they would face). But then instead of investigating the nature of discourse in the target situation, we launched directly into materials preparation. Time was short and uppermost in our minds was the need to have a set of materials ready for use in the English classes in the coming semester. The materials we produced largely consisted of comprehension activities on written texts on arts and design-related topics (for example, a description of an arts movement from the art history textbook the students used) and sets of what we considered 'arts-related' vocabulary (such as, lists of shapes and colours). We also selected a general English grammar course book to use alongside our 'Arts and Design' materials. However, we did not investigate the features of language use in the Arts and Design studies.

With hindsight, the 'solution' (the course and materials) we created had shortcomings. We knew relatively little about discourse in the kinds of texts the students would be reading, listening to or writing, or the nature of the interaction in the speaking events in which they would participate. The texts and activities we selected and designed as course materials were related to the interests of the students in terms of broad topic areas. The grammar focus of the course was general (we had not, for example, identified grammatical structures or patterns that occurred with any particular frequency in the discourse in the area) and the vocabulary focus represented a layman's view of what might be important in this field.

One key 'speaking' event for the students of Arts and Design was the 'jury'. Having produced a design or work of art, the student would be required to attend a jury in which the student would answer questions and defend the work. The juries were 'open house' and any number of students and faculty could attend. This event involved a specific type of discourse (for example, responding to criticisms). Before we ran the English course the first time, we knew little about this discourse. We could have observed and possibly recorded some juries in order to investigate the discourse involved. But we did not, although we did learn more about the discourse at a later date.

Scenario 2

The second scenario illustrates a situation in which an EAP teacher/course developer launched directly into empirical research with insufficient regard for the considerable body of information available in the literature. The situation was a university EGAP programme for students from a range of disciplines. The EGAP course in question was Academic Listening, a course the students took in their first year of undergraduate study while concurrently taking courses in their own departments. Needs analysis showed that the students found it difficult to follow lectures in their own departments (subject areas). The teacher was asked to develop an academic listening course to address this need.

The teacher conducted further needs analysis and identified that a major problem for the students was following topic development and topic shifts in lectures. The teacher decided to investigate 'lecture discourse' by collecting authentic lectures and examining the discourse in them to identify how the lecturers introduced and signalled topics and topic shifts. The teacher planned to use the results of the investigation of the discourse (the description) in the materials for the Academic Listening course. For the next three months the teacher went to a great deal of trouble arranging and making recordings of lectures in a range of departments across the university. Once made, the recordings were then transcribed, a time-consuming task. The teacher duly set about studying the transcripts and identifying the markers and signals of topic change and shifts. In time, the teacher drew up a list of the lexical expressions the lecturers used to change the topic and this description was included in the course materials along with some awareness-raising tasks to focus students' attention on these particular features in academic discourse.

All of this took a considerable amount of time, effort and resources. Yet already in existence at the time of the investigation were corpora that included authentic academic lectures from a range of disciplines, corpora that can be accessed (and were set up partly for the purpose of use) by other researchers and teachers. These included the British Academic Spoken English (BASE) corpus,[1] the Michigan Corpus of Academic Spoken English (MICASE),[2] and the Wellington Corpus of Spoken English (Holmes, Vine and Johnson, 1998). The BASE corpus comprises in excess of 150 monologic lectures from a range of disciplinary areas including Humanities, Social Sciences, Life Sciences and Physical Sciences. Moreover, there was already a body of literature reporting research into topic signals and markers of topic shift in lectures and which could inform pedagogy. For a recent review of this literature, see Thompson (2003). In short, the investigation by the EAP teacher in this example covered largely well-trodden ground.

A good deal of research into specialist discourse has been conducted, although the areas of research interest are uneven. Investigation of text and discourse has been the focus of the great majority of research articles in *English for Specific Purposes* since its inception in 1980 (Master, 2005). However, some areas of ESP have received more research interest than others. EAP is one area that has received a good deal of research interest, especially in regard to written discourse. Discourse and communication in industrial workplaces has received less research interest than that in professional settings (Roberts, 2005 p. 121). In ESP-oriented publications, studies of written discourse generally outnumber those on spoken discourse (Master, 2005).

In summary, before leaping into either course design or collection of empirical data, ESP teachers and course developers can usefully consider the following related questions.

- What language (skills, genres and features) do the learners need to know?
- Is information (data and descriptions) about these already available?

- If not, how can the ESP course developers collect data and investigate these?
- If so, how can the already available data and/or descriptions be used to supplement or replace the course developers' investigation?

3.3 Approaches to investigation of specialist communication

The previous section argued that it is not always necessary for ESP teachers and course developers to conduct their own empirical investigations of specialist discourse. But sometimes they do need to.[3] Thus they need to be familiar with approaches to investigating specialist discourse. Hüttner, Smit and Mehlmauer-Larcher (2009) make a case for this. These writers report that in Austria, ESP is an obligatory subject for the majority of students attending vocational upper-secondary school and colleges and it involves a very wide range of specializations. Over a lifetime of ESP teaching, the teachers need to be able to teach many different ESP subjects, including unfamiliar and newly emerging genres. Since it is not possible to predict which genres future ESP teachers may find themselves teaching, ESP teacher education should enable practitioners to 'autonomously analyse any ESP genre with a view to teaching it' (p. 100). I would suspect that ESP teachers in a number of other countries are similarly expected over the course of their professional lives to be able to analyse discourse in any number of ESP areas and genres.

This section briefly introduces three important approaches to investigating specialist discourse. These are ethnography, genre analysis and corpus analysis. Both genre and corpus analysis can be considered as forms of text analysis since both use texts as the primary type of data and both construct descriptions on the basis of observations of patterns or features in these texts. In reality, approaches can be and often are combined.

3.3.1 Ethnography

Ethnography is a form of qualitative research. Qualitative research has been described as study of phenomena in their natural settings, attempting to make sense of, or to interpret, phenomena in terms of the meanings people bring to them (Denzin and Lincoln, 2000, p. 3).

Ethnographies are in-depth and situated investigations, generally focusing on a specific setting such as one programme or institution. Ethnographies seek to describe the behaviour of a particular group and to understand it from the perspectives of members of that group (Richards, 2003, p. 14). The researcher often spends a prolonged period of time in the field (setting) to gather rich information about the context, the participants and their understandings of events, such as, speaking situations in their everyday world. This information is used to help the analyst interpret the events from the participants' perspectives.

Ethnographers select from a range of data collection methods including open-ended interviews, narrative accounts, observations and documents as sources of data. Having collected the data, the investigator stands back from them and tries to interpret what the events mean to the participants. Creswell (2003) suggests steps researchers can follow once the qualitative data has been collected: organize and prepare the data (for example, transcribing interviews and typing up field notes); read through all the data and get a general sense of the information – perhaps write notes in margins or record general thoughts about it; make a more detailed analysis including segmenting data into categories and labelling them with a term, often a term used by one or more participants; and using the categories to generate a small number of themes.

A study by Northcott (2001) illustrates an ethnographic approach. The study investigated lectures on an MBA programme in a UK university setting in preparation for the development for a new ESP course for MBA students. The study focused specifically on the role of interactive lecturing styles (participatory lectures in which students are encouraged to contribute orally) and set out to identify ways in which these styles might be problematic for L2 learners (p. 19). The researcher carried out a lengthy period of observation of lectures to identify ways different lecturers accomplished an interactive style. The strategy of one lecturer, for example, was to allow question pauses during the lecture so that students could ask questions individually while the others had a break. By observing the interaction and discourse in the lectures, the researcher was able to identify ways these types of lectures could be problematic for the non-native English-speaking students. For example, listening and understanding other students' contributions as well as the lecturer implied greater demands in terms of cognitive and phonological processing. Difficulties could also arise when other students made contributions involving culturally bound content (some contributions, for example, seemed to require background political knowledge of the UK).

For further reading on qualitative research methods in TESOL including ethnography see Chapelle and Duff (2003) and Richards (2003).

3.3.2 Genre analysis

The term 'genre analysis' has already been used a good deal in this book and it is arguably the most influential approach to the analysis of language use in ESP to date. Following the seminal work by Swales (1990, 2004), other researchers including Bhatia (1993, 2004) have developed and adapted this approach.

Genres are types of texts, such as academic lectures or conference abstracts, nursing care plans, sales' letters or news reports. The texts in a genre set have a common function or set of functions, are often organized in conventional ways and use similar linguistic features. Each discourse community a person participates in has a set of genres that are essential to its function and work, genres that its members either produce or receive. A genre label is the name given to the text type by the members of the community in question and the members of that community similarly perceive the genre's function or functions and they share expectations about how the genre is written (or spoken). In Parks' study (2001) that was described in section 3.1 we saw that a key genre for the nursing community was the 'nursing care plan'.

A genre can be described as the way people in a specific community typically get things done through written or spoken discourse (Paltridge, 2006, p. 84). Genre analysis aims to identify patterns underlying specific genres (text types), such as nursing care plans. It seeks to identify how particular social groups (often termed discourse communities) conventionally organize specific types of texts (genres) to accomplish their aims (communicative purposes). In this approach, samples of the genre (for example, sample nursing care plans) are collected. The analyst seeks to identify features common to these samples and to investigate the context of use in order to understand why the genre is the way it is. The description that results from genre analysis is often very revealing for others including those struggling to produce (or understand) the genre themselves.

If we consider the 'conference abstract', for example, we might say that it is a genre produced by and for the academic community, and that it functions to provide a synopsis of the paper that will be given, and to attract an audience to the paper. If we collect samples of such abstracts (for example, from the programmes from various conferences in Language Teaching) and then set about examining them, we will probably begin to observe a number of commonalities in terms of what kind of content is included by the Language Teaching community and how it is organized. We may also make observations of language use. We may observe, for example, that adjectives are infrequently used. We might wish to compare two sets of texts. For example, Agathopoulou (2009) used genre analysis to compare abstracts submitted to applied and theoretical linguistics conferences in Greece. She organized the abstracts into two sets, those that were high-rated by the selection committee and those that were low-rated. The researcher then compared the genre features of the two sets.

Paltridge (2006, p. 98) describes steps used in genre analysis, saying the steps can be used selectively according to the purpose of the analysis and how much is already known about genre. The starting point can be either text first or context first. The analyst either begins by examining samples of the genre and looking for typical patterns of discourse in them or begins by investigating the context first to find out about the functions of the genre according to the discourse community that produces it and the values and expectations they have for it. The analyst searches for prior knowledge on the genre (existing literature including guide books, manuals and practitioner advice and research reports). The analyst makes definitions of the speaker (or writer) and audience of the genre and the relationship between them, the overall function(s) of the genre, its subject matter and how the genre is used within a network of other genres. The analyst collects samples of the genre (texts). The analyst may select a single typical text (genre exemplar) and conduct a detailed analysis of its structure and content (the moves), or the analyst may examine a greater number of texts if investigating a particular linguistic feature.

The study by Ding (2007) illustrates a genre-based approach. The genre in question was the 'personal statement' (the accompanying letter) in an application for graduate study to medical and dental schools. According to the researcher, applicants are generally unfamiliar with the conventions of the genre and know little about expectations held for it by the target discourse community (the selection committee at the graduate dental and medical schools), and although college writing teachers are often asked to help students prepare such letters, very limited research and description of this genre has been available.

The researcher set about investigating the context such as word limitations, advice in guidebooks, and also interviewed professors in charge of admissions at two medical schools to elicit their expectations for the personal statement. The professors expected, for example, that the letters would include evidence of commitment to medicine/dentistry and a discussion of specific, first-hand experiences of helping people.

The investigator collected samples of personal statements for medical and dental schools available on public websites and used these for analysis. The analysis revealed a common five-move sequence (*explaining the reason to pursue the proposed study, establishing credentials related to the field of medicine/dentistry, discussing relevant life experience, stating future career goals* and *describing personality*). The study also revealed the options (sub moves or 'steps') used by individual writers to make the moves. For example, writers drew on any of three possible steps in making the first move (explaining reasons). These steps were *explaining academic/intellectual interests, describing understanding the field* and *explaining personal/family experiences*. Ding compared the moves and steps in the texts that had been posted on the websites as successful or unsuccessful examples. The study also involved the use of corpus analysis. Once the moves were identified, Ding used computer software to investigate frequently occurring words in the two sets of texts.

3.3.3   Corpus analysis

Corpus analysis techniques allow investigators to identify patterns in a body of data of language use. A corpus is a collection of authentic written or spoken texts available electronically and which can therefore be accessed with computer software (such as, concordancing software). The texts can be representative of a language variety (for example, written and spoken New Zealand English) or of a specific field (Academic English or Business English). It is also possible to make a small corpus of texts for a specific investigation (such as, Ding's corpus of application letters to dental and medical graduate schools). Small corpora do not aim to represent language use as a whole, but allow for a specific focus with obvious advantages for ESP-oriented investigations (Hüttner et al., 2009).

The focus of a corpus analysis can be identification of specific linguistic features. The analysis could, for example, seek to identify complex noun phrases in academic written or spoken texts (to see how and where the noun phrases occur in the discourse). Or it could seek to identify commonly occurring words in the corpus (to make a word list) or to identify words typically occurring together (to make a list of collocations). Many readers will be familiar with the typical ways of presenting the results of corpus-based analyses of collocations through concordances. Table 3.1 shows concordances from a small corpus of discussion sections of journal articles in Language Teaching which were collected and analysed by the writer using Wmatrix (Rayson, 2009). The corpus was investigated for words in the semantic category 'research' (Archer, Wilson and Rayson, 2002). Table 3.2 shows the number of 'research'-related words evident in the corpus. The word 'research' was the most frequently used item in this category. It was used 34 times.

In recent years the concept of frequency in corpus-based analyses has come under scrutiny and writers such as Baker (2006) have developed the notion of 'keyness'.

> It is possible to compare the frequencies in one wordlist against another in order to determine which words occur statistically more often in wordlist A when compared to wordlist B and vice versa. Then all the words that do occur more often than expected in one file, when compared to another are compiled together into another list, called a keyword list. And it is this keyword list which is likely to be more useful in suggesting lexical items that could warrant further examination. A keyword list therefore gives a measure of saliency, whereas a simple word list only provides frequency. (Baker, 2006, p. 125)

We could, for example, construct two comparable corpora (discussion sections of articles and dissertations in Language Teaching). We could then use corpus analytical techniques to make word frequency lists of each corpus and then create a keyword list showing the words more salient in the writing of either group (the writers of published research articles and the student writers of the dissertations).

3.4   Summary

This chapter has argued that descriptions of specialist discourse are at the heart of ESP course design. The chapter discussed where such descriptions come

Table 3.1 Concordances from semantic category of 'research'

Left context	Node	Right context
me measure of comprehension to	examine	how comprehension of the dictog
g in progress , as a number of	researchers	has suggested , then the findin
LREs . Furthermore , a closer	analysis	of the data for the HL pairs re
(in the L1 or L2) , whereas	research based	on developmental readiness conc
n of grammar problems , future	research	could employ measures to examin
earch could employ measures to	examine	if LREs promote noticing of for
texts) . In addition , future	research	could also employ dyad specific
, Swain and Lapkin , 1998) or	analyse	learners uptake of specific for
erhaps it may be worthwhile to	examine	LREs across different tasks inv
oficiency . That said , future	research	could use a variety of more obj
ungHee Sheen Language Teaching	Research	8 , 3 (2004) ; pp. 263300 V D
and repair were observable and	analysable	on a discourse level , using a
le 1 for details) . The first	research	question asked the extent to wh
her reports from focus-on-form	research	in communicatively oriented cla
s et al. , 2001) . The second	research	question asked how learner upta
chers correct form . The third	research	question addressed the extent t
On the other hand , a post hoc	analysis	shows that the recasts that occ
rehensive review of the recast	research	, conclude that recasts are mos
ewen (2003) reports from his	investigation	of L2 communicative classrooms
, there is an obvious need to	investigate	differences within individual i
in line with those of previous	researchers	(Duff and Polio , 1990 ; Gearo
e results that emerge from the	analysis	of the interactional goals of t
andro Benati Language Teaching	Research	9,1 (2005) ; pp. 6793 VI Disc
f this study was formulated to	investigate	the effects of PI , a type of T
upport previous findings on PI	research	that indicated that PI is succe
second question of this study	sought	to investigate the effects of t
estion of this study sought to	investigate	the effects of the three treatm
t the main results of previous	research	on PI , which showed that the P
ned by the majority of studies	investigating	the effects of PI , which show

Table 3.2 Words from semantic category of 'research'

research	34
analysis	16
researchers	6
monitoring	4
examine	4
investigate	3
monitored	3
investigating	2
investigated	2
checked	2
analysable	1
sought	1
analyse	1
researcher	1
looked_into	1
research_based	1
search	1
seeking	1
empirical	1
investigation	1

from – searches of the existing literature and/or teachers and course developers conducting their own empirical investigations. The chapter has reminded teachers/course developers that texts, corpora and descriptions of specialist discourse may already be available. They may not need to start from scratch with their investigation, and as advised by Rapley (2007, pp. 8–9), should bear in mind data that already exists as well as data that needs to be generated. Nevertheless ESP teachers and course developers often do need to collect and investigate primary data. The chapter introduced three approaches to investigation (ethnography, genre analysis and corpus analysis).

3.5 Discussion

1. Burns and Moore (2008) investigated questioning in simulations of consultations between accountants and clients. The examples of investigations of specialist discourse described earlier in this chapter involved the collection of authentic language use (in the form of authentic texts or recordings of naturally occurring talk). However, there are some situations in which it is very difficult or even impossible to collect such data or samples of language use. On occasion investigators turn to alternative means of gathering data. One option is for investigators to elicit samples of language use. In regard to spoken events or genres, this could involve the use of simulations or role plays. Burns and Moore discuss the use of simulations when ESP teachers

cannot get access to spoken data from actual workplace settings and report how they used simulations of accountant–client consultations. Participants in the simulations were acquaintances of the researchers and Masters of Accountancy students, and a set of scenarios was devised. One scenario involved the 'accountant' explaining to the 'client' how to complete an income tax return.

Select a spoken genre important to the needs of a workplace-focused ESP class you teach or may teach in the future. If you were unable to obtain access to the workplace setting and were also unable to find relevant literature on the genre, would you consider using simulations to obtain language data and if so how might you set these up?

2. As stated earlier in this chapter, investigations of specialist discourse may involve a combination of approaches. Flowerdew and Wan (2006) used genre analysis to investigate 'computation letters' written by tax accountants in an accountancy firm in Hong Kong and supplemented this with ethnographic enquiry to find out why the accountants wrote the letters the way they did.

One typical combination is the use of ethnography (*before* the collection of texts, such as, video or audio recordings) of a particular spoken event or genre. Two 'ethnographic fieldwork' options are described by Rapley (2007, p. 44). The two options are carrying out a series of visits to the site of the investigation and shadowing someone in their job. Such measures give investigators a sense of what texts they will need for their investigation and indicate the limitations of what texts alone will show (and, therefore, what will need to be found out through other means, such as interviews). Investigators can use this initial period of fieldwork to find out about the participants' work routines and practices, whether it is possible to obtain copies of documents used by the participants at work, when and where the spoken or written genres of interest occur and whether the participants use specialized or complex language in these genres (Rapley, 2007, p. 44).

Think of a spoken or written genre that you might investigate in your own teaching or learning context. Make a plan for an initial period of fieldwork. What would your fieldwork involve and what information would you hope to obtain?

3. This chapter has argued that it can be useful to consider descriptions and research of specialist discourse that already exist before embarking on an empirical investigation. Some possible sources of literature, descriptions and data have already been mentioned in this chapter. These and some other potential sources are listed below:

- corpora, recordings and transcripts
- manuals and guides to writing

- practitioner advice (such as, guidelines)
- official documents (such as, leaflets and workplace protocols)
- websites
- resource banks on vocational education, such as, Workplace English Language and Literacy Program Australia, Workbase New Zealand and Career and Vocational Education US and Canada (Roberts, 2005, p. 122)
- research articles – key journals in ESP are *English for Specific Purposes* and the *Journal of English for Academic Purposes*. *Applied Linguistics, TESOL Quarterly* and *English Language Teaching Journal* sometimes publish studies in this area
- books and chapters in books on discourse in specific areas.

In relation to the spoken or written genre you discussed in Question 2 discuss how you would set about searching for literature, data and description that may already exist.

Notes

1. The British Academic Spoken English (BASE) corpus was developed at the Universities of Warwick and Reading under the directorship of Hilary Nesi and Paul Thompson. Corpus development was assisted by funding from BALEAP, EURALEX, the British Academy and the Arts and Humanities Research Council, http://www2.warwick. ac.uk/fac/soc/celte/research/base.
2. The Michigan Corpus of Academic Spoken English (MICASE) is an online, searchable collection of transcripts of academic speech events recorded at the University of Michigan, http://www.hti.umich.edu/m/micase/.
3. Investigators may be required to make a formal application to an ethics committee at their school or university. They may need to provide participant information and consent sheets. Prospective researchers should consult their respective institutions in this regard.

4

Developing the Curriculum

Chapter 3 described the kinds of investigations teachers and course developers carry out when they wish to obtain information about language use in a specialist area. At some point, decisions have to be made about the ESP course itself – Who is the course for and what will it focus on? What will the syllabus contain and what types of instruction and materials will it provide? How can the course be evaluated?

Decisions about course design do not necessarily follow the kinds of investigations of specialist discourse described in the preceding chapter, but rather may precede them. The course developer may decide on an item of course content and then seek out descriptions of language use for it. On the other hand, as described in Chapter 3, investigations of specialist discourse may suggest ideas for course design. For example, a course developer reads an article describing discourse in academic lectures. The article makes the developer aware of features of lecture discourse (such as, signals of topic change and asides) that would be useful to include in the syllabus for the academic listening skills course.

This chapter discusses considerations in course design and materials development that are of particular importance in ESP. Curriculum development per se is a very broad topic and one that is addressed in the literature on general language teaching. The present work does not set out to cover this broad topic but instead sets out to examine specific features of ESP curriculum development. Accordingly, the chapter examines aspects in ESP course development and introduces a number of dichotomies related to this including *wide- and narrow-angled course designs, real and carrier content and authentic and non-authentic texts.*

4.1 Focusing the course

4.1.1 Wide- and narrow-angled course designs

A point of departure for course development is determining who the course is for (the target group of learners). From this decision, other decisions follow, including determining what the course will focus on and its content. One of the key issues in ESP course development is the question of how specific the course should be in terms of target audience. A distinction is drawn between courses that are 'wide angled' (designed for a more general group of learners) and those that are 'narrow angled' (designed for a very specific group of learners). Courses titled EGAP and Business English can be considered 'wide angled' since they are designed for classes focused on broad academic skills or a register (Business English) which encompasses many subfields including marketing, accounting and management. Courses titled English for Nursing Studies and English for Accountants can be considered relatively 'narrow angled' since they refer to courses that are more specific, as they have been designed for learners we might assume have largely homogeneous needs and who have a particular type of academic or work environment in mind. Furthermore, courses can be even more specific. For example, accountants often distinguish between two areas, financial accountancy and management accountancy, and a course could be developed for just one of these sub areas – English for Financial Accountancy or English for Management Accountancy. Some ESP courses are developed for groups of learners with very similar needs and some for learners with only somewhat similar needs. Some ESP courses are developed for disciplines or occupations as broad fields and some for specialities within them.

In practical terms, determining the focus of a course may be based on findings from needs analysis. We may find a clear divide, for example, between health care professionals who need to develop their oral communication skills for dealing with patients and those who need to develop their written communication for various types of reports. But the choice of a wide- or narrow-angled course design can also be based on decisions about grouping learners. For example, if 30 health professionals were to come to a language school, which approach would be better: to divide them into three groups according to proficiency levels and teach a wide-angled English Skills for Health Professionals or Medical English course at all three levels, or to group them according to their roles in the health care sector, perhaps nurses in one group, physiotherapists in another and medical doctors in the third? In the latter case, we could teach a narrow set of language skills and focus on specific areas of language use (for example, the ability to describe movement and function is very important for physiotherapists). Where would we place the 'others' such as the two radiotherapists and the one pharmacist who are also coming to the school? What if the needs of the doctors are diverse and the 'clinicians' in the group feel they have few language needs in common with the 'physicians' in the group?

There are theoretical considerations as well as practical ones. One consideration is the notion of general varieties of language. Is there such an entity as 'Medical English' and, if so, might descriptions of it be simply too broad to be of much interest to any of our health care practitioners? Similarly, are there entities such as Business English and Academic English and, if so, are descriptions of them too general to interest people working in different branches of business and students from their various disciplines? Hyland (2008) questions the 'widely held assumption that there is a single core vocabulary for academic study irrespective of discipline' (p. 113) and has argued that 'while generic labels such as "academic English" or "scientific English" may be a convenient shorthand for describing a general variety, they conceal a wealth of discursive complexity'. In relation to EAP, Hyland (2002a) maintains:

> The discourses of the academy do not form an undifferentiated, unitary mass but a variety of subject-specific literacies. Disciplines have different views of knowledge, different research practices, and different ways of seeing the world, and as a result, investigating the practices of those disciplines will inevitably take us into greater specificity. (p. 390)

A second theoretical consideration is the notion of generic skills. Is there a set of 'generic' skills that is transferable across different roles in the health care sector or business? For EAP, a similar question can be asked. Is there a set of generic academic skills relevant to the needs of students in a range of disciplines? Some writers (e.g. Jordan, 1997) identify a set of generic academic skills (such as, writing summaries and taking notes in lectures) and consider these to be much the same across disciplines. A major premise for a wide-angled course design is the idea of the transferability of skills – the students will transfer the knowledge and skills they gain from the wide-angled course (such as, EGAP or English for Business Skills) to their own specific area (such as, their studies in psychology or law, or their work in management or marketing). But do students transfer these? The second theoretical consideration concerns the value of descriptions of language use in a broad domain such as Academic English or Business English. We can argue that the learners will need to use language not in a broad domain but in their specific discipline or type of work. So why not provide them with descriptions of language use in these specific disciplines or types of work rather than a more general description of potentially limited relevance? Is language use in various 'related' business disciplines, such as management and marketing, or various health care fields such as medicine and nursing, similar? Hyland (2004, p. 151) critiques wide-angled options arguing that different disciplines can have their own ways of crafting arguments, reflecting different ideas about what is of value and how it can be communicated.

This issue has been discussed in relation to second language writing instruction. Ferris (2001, p. 300) remarks, 'One of the most persistent and controversial issues in L2 writing is the debate over the purposes of EAP classes. Should teachers aim to develop generalised academic writing skills in their students, hoping that these skills and strategies will transfer to subsequent writing tasks across the curriculum? Or should they focus instead on teaching students how to analyze and imitate the norms of specific discourse communities to which the students hope to gain admission?' The development of wide-angled EGAP courses, according to Hyland (2002a), reflects the unwillingness of universities to fund the development of highly specific narrow-angled courses.

The terms 'wide- and narrow-angled' course designs might suggest a two-way divide. However, courses can be more or less narrow or wide and can be seen as existing on a continuum of specificity. At one end of this continuum are the most general ESP courses, courses that focus on a register, such as Business English or Academic English and courses that focus on a generic set of skills in an area, such as Business English Skills or EGAP. Towards the other end of the continuum are courses focusing on specific needs and language use of a particular area of work or study, for example, English for Accountants (and the narrower option, English for Financial Accountants), or English for Social Science Studies (and the narrower option, English for Sociology Studies). Some ESP courses are devised for a very specific group of learners, for instance, English for Auditors (auditing is a branch of financial accounting) and an even narrower option, a course organized at the behest of a particular workplace or division within a workplace, for example, a course for the financial accountants in the auditing division of a particular accountancy firm. See the representation of courses that range from low to high specificity shown in Figure 4.1

Wide angled

1a. Business   English
1b. Business English   Skills
2a.   English   for   Accountants
2b.   English for Financial Accountants
3a.   English for Financial Auditors

3b   English for Financial Auditors
                    at Xco.

Narrow angled

Figure 4.1 The wide- and narrow-angled continuum

The course design options shown in Figure 4.1 are examined below. Arguments can be made for all options shown in this figure. To a large extent, determining the focus of an ESP course (more or less wide or narrow angled) depends largely on circumstances. Belcher (2006) argues that for many ESP practitioners the wide versus narrow approach debate is a 'nonissue because instructional decisions should have more to do with the learners themselves than with instructor preference or beliefs – undergraduate students without majors may suggest a wide-angled approach and postgraduate students such as nurses and pilots may suggest a narrow-angled approach' (p. 139). Often what drives the decision about course design is the situation in which teachers/course designers find themselves. If the students are a fairly homogeneous group in relation to their target needs, then a course towards the narrow-angled end of the continuum is not only feasible but is almost inevitable. But when highly specific options are not feasible, is everything lost? The following discussion describes options along the wide- and narrow-angled continuum represented in Figure 4.1 and explores their possible advantages and disadvantages. It is based on discussion in a previous work (Basturkmen, 2003).

Level 1: Wide-angled

Level 1a courses focus on a variety of language such as, Business English or Academic English. They are not based on an analysis of needs of a particular group of learners but on description of language use in a field or discipline. Learners do not necessarily need a high level of proficiency in English for a course such as this. They can learn the basic forms (the 'common core') of a language through a specific variety as well as through the usual 'language classroom variety' (Bloor and Bloor, 1986, p. 19). Level 1b courses focus on a set of generic skills such as writing skills in Business English.

Level 1 type courses have some advantages. They can be developed to cater for a range of learners including post-, pre- or during-experience learners. Learners may enjoy topics and texts in the general area of interest, not just topics and texts from their own specific area. For example, a student of sociology may be interested in topics from psychology and somebody working in management may be interested in topics from marketing and finance. On the other hand, Johns and Dudley-Evans (1991) argue that while the wide-angled approach may be suitable in some circumstances, it is not suitable in others, such as for graduate students and professionals.

Level 2

Level 2 courses focus on the needs of a fairly specific groups of learners. We might assume that the needs of learners in 2a are rather more heterogeneous than those of learners in 2b type courses. Arguments for basing courses on needs analysis have been examined in Chapter 2. Compared to Level 3 courses, Level 2 courses are advantageous in terms of practicality and economy – different courses do not need to be developed for each and every group.

Some disadvantages can also be mentioned. Level 2 courses, based as they are on the perceived communicative needs in target disciplines of study or workplaces, are often unsuitable for learners with limited proficiency. Communicative needs in disciplines and workplaces are generally linguistically complex and thus demand a certain level of language proficiency. For example, writing in a profession or a discipline generally requires a fairly extensive vocabulary and knowledge of grammatical structures as well as familiarity with genres and conventions of communication.

The fact that Level 2 courses are not highly specific may mean the content is insufficiently focused. Discourse may vary in different branches of professional work and in different subjects in a disciplinary area. Flowerdew and Wan (2006) offer a description of tax computation letters, a genre that is expected to be of great interest to accountants specializing in taxation but of much less interest to accountants working in other areas. An investigation of the writing requirements on a postgraduate environmental studies programme in a US university (Samraj, 2002) revealed considerable variation across the requirements of particular courses. For example, 'term papers' were required in the Wildlife Behaviour and Resource Policy courses, but the actual requirements of the papers differed. Wildlife Behaviour term papers required students to select a topic and review previous research, hypotheses and suggestions for future research on that topic. Resource Policy term papers required students to compose memos based on workplace simulations. Samraj's study showed just how much variation can exist within one discipline since one course required an 'academic' genre and the other a 'workplace' genre. Samraj argues that EAP teachers need to show students that academic writing does not only vary along disciplinary lines (p. 174).

Level 3: Narrow angled

Level 3 courses are tailored to the specific needs of a particular group of learners with the idea that course content will fit their needs very precisely and thus efficiently prepare them to meet the demands of their target situations.

The notion of specificity can be linked to a social constructivist perspective of language. According to this perspective, disciplines and professions are constructed and reproduced through their discursive practices and language is construed not as a general code but as form of situated action. Hyland (2002b) summarizes the tenets of this theory as follows:

> Language is not just a means for self-expression then, it is how we construct and sustain reality, and we do this as members of communities, using the language of those communities. The features of a text are therefore influenced

by the community for which it was written and so are best understood, and taught, through the specific genres of communities. (p. 41)

The perspective is reflected in many genre-based ESP course designs. In such designs genres are seen as the means by which the target discourse communities enact their everyday work and by which they are defined. Although members of these communities know how to reproduce these genres, their knowledge of the genres is often procedural or implicit rather than declarative or explicit, and the ESP course aims to make the knowledge explicit.

The focus on the communicative events in a particular group generally leads to a focus on the products of communication of the group. This contrasts to Type 1b courses which focus on a set of generic skills or processes (such as, writing or speaking processes). Master (1997b) describes the value of focusing on products in ESP saying:

> ESP shifted the overemphasis on process back to a legitimate concern for product, primarily because it reminded us that the world wants products and does not particularly care how they were created. The concept of genre analysis has shown us that there are prescribed forms for use in technical writing, and that in order to be accepted into the occupational subculture or discourse community, those forms must be adhered to. (p. 30)

We would expect that learners would find highly specific courses very motivating because they are designed to be clearly relevant to the learners' needs. However, this may not always be the case and students are not always as focused on the target situation as it may seem at first. Students change courses and workers change jobs and roles and few of the members of our narrow-angled ESP course may in fact end up studying or working in the situations for which the course was designed. A study of an ESP programme for care workers (Uvin, 1996) showed students had little interest in the course content focusing on the communicative needs of care workers since they were hoping to progress beyond these positions in the future.

There are other potential disadvantages of highly specific courses. Firstly, such courses can be argued to present a restricted language and thus only help learners function in very limited circumstances. They might be seen as a form of 'language training' that provides learners with surface linguistic forms conventionally used in target situations rather than 'language education' that provides knowledge of how the language works at a deep level and which is needed for the creative use of language (Widdowson, 1983). Secondly, students in narrow-angled ESP courses are not likely to have identical needs and at least some of the course content is bound to be more relevant to some individuals than others. Thirdly, the variety of roles in workplaces and courses in academic programmes is simply too diverse for any one ESP course to deal with in depth. Finally, the amount of research and preparation required for highly specific ESP course designs is considerable. Teachers and course developers need preparation time in which to investigate discourse and communication in a specific discipline or workplace. Access to workplaces can be problematic and members of disciplines and workplaces are busy people with limited time to discuss language use and communication. Although such investigations are of great value, there are probably only some situations when the amount of time and cost for research and preparation can be justified. These situations might be when the course will run more than once or twice and when courses are established at the behest of a particular workplace or group.

4.2 Determining course content

4.2.1 Real and carrier content

In ESP a distinction is drawn between real content and carrier content (Dudley-Evans and St John, 1998; Belcher, 2006). Real content denotes pedagogical aims, such as the features of language the learners will hopefully become more aware of or be better able to produce or the language skills they gain control of. Carrier content denotes, as its name suggests, the means of delivering the real content. These means include the use of texts or activities. For example, if we were teaching an ESP class for financial accountants, and if one of our pedagogic aims was to familiarize our learners with vocabulary used in financial reporting, we might use a company's annual report as a text to 'carry' the content of interest. Figure 4.2 shows part of the Financial Review section of a company annual report (Fletcher Building, 2009). This text could be used as carrier content in an ESP class focusing on vocabulary related to finance. In the lesson, students may be asked to read the text and identify how the items 'cash', 'capital' and 'debt' are used. For example, they could be asked to discuss the meaning of collocations involving 'capital', such as 'capital expenditure', 'capital raising' and 'capital notes'.

Alternatively, we might use a combination of texts as carrier content. For example, we might develop an integrated skills activity in which students read company annual reports and make notes on the types of assets (intellectual, physical and financial) listed. The students could use the notes to prepare an oral report. See the example simulation activity in Figure 4.3

4.2.2 Planning the syllabus

A major consideration in planning a syllabus is the question of what content should be included in the course. The following discussion considers the selection of 'real' content (as discussed in Figure 4.2) and how findings from needs analysis (as discussed in Chapter 2) can be brought to bear in this task. How the course has been focused impacts on what will be included in the syllabus. For

Cashflow and capital expenditure

Cashflow from operations was $533 million compared with $434 million in the prior year. The strong improvement in cashflow was largely attributable to a focus on working capital management with $203 million in cash generated from reduced debtors and $101 million from lower inventory levels. Cashflow also benefited from the sale of the head office building in Auckland for $36 million.

Capital expenditure for the year was $289 million compared with $349 million in the prior year. This level of expenditure reflected the carry-over of $168 million of projects from the prior year, with $121 million of new capital expenditure approved during the year. Significant projects included construction of the new metal roofing plant in Hungary; the new port cement facility in Auckland; installation of the redeployed HPL press in Formica Finland; and the purchase of additional sand and quarry reserves in Australia by Rocla Quarries.

A total of $246 million was distributed to shareholders and minority interests.

The company's guidelines on future dividend declarations require consideration of available cash after allowing for growth requirements and a prudent gearing level.

Capital management and funding

Balance sheet gearing (net debt to net debt plus equity) at 31.1 percent decreased from 40.1 percent at 30 June 2008, reflecting the equity raising of $526 in April 2009. Approximately 87 percent of all borrowings have fixed interest rates with an average duration of 5.2 years and at a rate of 7.20 percent. Inclusive of the floating rate borrowings, the average rate of debt is currently 7.42 percent.

The company remains in a strong financial position and is comfortably within all its relevant debt covenants.

Interest cover (EBIT to total interest paid) was 4.0 times, compared to 5.6 times at 30 June 2008.

Net debt decreased by $496 million to $1,350 million at 30 June 2009, again largely due to the capital raising. The company had undrawn committed bank funding available of $1,142 million at June 2009 compared to $378 million in the prior year.

Two series of capital notes totalling $131 million were issued during the year with $83 million of notes remaining as treasury stock.

Debt requiring refinancing within the next 12 months is around $110 million, including $75 million of capital notes subject to interest rate and term reset, and $25 million of expiring undrawn facilities.

Figure 4.2   Section from a company annual report as sample authentic text
Source: Page 29 of the *Financial Review of Fletcher Building Annual Report 2009*

In this simulation you will work in groups of three. Each of you takes the role of an accountant working to advise an overseas investor who is considering buying shares in the Australasian Banking sector. The investor is looking into three banks. Your aim is to identify how each bank reports its assets and value.

Read the annual report from one of the three banks. Make notes on the physical, financial, intellectual and 'other' property listed in the report. (What items are listed under each area and how is each valued?)

Attend a meeting in which each of you firstly reports your findings and then jointly prepare a short written report for the client on your joint findings.

Figure 4.3   Simulation activity using authentic texts

example, as Belcher (2006) explains, if the focus of the course is wide-angled EGAP, we might decide to teach the most common academic words.

A syllabus is generally organized in units. The units might be construed as areas of grammar and/or vocabulary, genres, language functions (speech acts), notions, skills or strategies. The course might involve a combination of types of units (Basturkmen, 2006). An example of such a combination is shown in Cowling (2007). Cowling describes how findings from a needs analysis were used to plan the syllabus for a series of workplace-based courses in Japan. The needs analysis involved multiple methods and sources of information and suggested that the course needed to provide a communicative component in which students would be able to adapt their current general English into English knowledge for business situations. The course also needed to consider cultural issues in communication with foreign business people and provide realistic or authentic samples of language use (Cowling, p. 434). These requirements suggested a syllabus that was partly content based and included a cultural focus. For example, one unit in the course is titled 'Describing Products and Services'. The syllabus specifies discourse/language items for this unit (such as, the notions of weights and measures and the function of 'giving opinions'), content items (such as, 'engaging the customer' and 'presenting selling points') and cultural content on 'directness' and 'gestures' (p. 438).

In planning the syllabus, teachers/course developers make decisions about what to include in terms of:

- types of units
  such as: skills, vocabulary, genres, functions, notions and disciplinary, professional or cultural content
- items in the units
  such as: which genres, semantic sets and functions
- sequencing – what should come first, second and so forth and decisions made according to considerations
  such as: immediate and less immediate need, level of difficulty with easier items before more difficult items and logical flow – for instance, in Business English, opening meetings before closing meetings.

Needs analysis plays an important role in determining course content in ESP but it is not necessarily the only consideration. Parkinson et al. (2007) report the development of a reading and writing course for foundation year students in a South African University. The course focuses on developing academic literacies and, as Table 4.1 shows, is organized around four genres including the laboratory report and the essay. The report explains the choices made by the course developers. The developers were guided in part by findings from needs analysis (a previous study into the writing and reading tasks assigned to undergraduate science students by Jackson, Meyer and Parkinson (2006)) which showed that laboratory reports were the major type of writing assignment and the students were mainly assigned readings from textbooks. The developers were also guided, however, by theoretical considerations such as the value of integrating reading and writing – 'it is only when students read with comprehension that they can write effectively' (p. 446) and the role of 'scaffolding' based on ideas in the literature

Table 4.1   Examples of 'Communication in Science' topics

	Source materials	Literacies which are the focus of each topic include:
1. A poster on Marine Conservation	Popular science articles adapted from various sources including *National Geographic, Metrobeat* and the Internet	• Reading and comprehension • Analysis of a focused topic • Taking notes from a written source • Integrating information from multiple sources • Summarizing • Word processing • Using own sentences to avoid plagiarism
2. A laboratory report on varying the strength of an electromagnet	Extracts from an O-level textbook and two level 1 textbooks	• Designing and conducting an experiment • Recording measurements as tables and graphs • Learning features of the different parts of the Report genre
3. Essay on a range of solid waste disposal methods applied to the student's own community	A science journal article and popular journal articles	• Integrating information from multiple sources • Describing the environmental situation in the student's own community • Applying information to community's needs • Making a recommendation • Referencing
4. Oral presentation on Malaria	Popular journal articles and textbooks	• Preparing and presenting a talk to an audience: includes key cards and visual support

Source: Parkinson et al. (2007), p. 448

on sociocultural theory. The writers define scaffolding as the support offered by one who has mastered an activity to help another carry out the activity which would be too difficult if initially attempted on his or her own (p. 444).

4.3   Developing materials

4.3.1   Authentic and non-authentic texts

One of the key characteristics of ESP is that teachers and course developers value the use of authentic texts and tasks. The term 'authentic' denotes that the texts were written for purposes other than language teaching and learning. For example, should we be developing a course for financial accountants, we would probably try to include texts written by accountants and those in related financial sectors (such as, the financial section of a company annual report shown in Figure 4.2). Texts written by journalists could possibly be used if they were written for the purposes of communicating financial or economic ideas and information. We might also include tasks replicating those accountants in the workplace might carry out, such as reading a company annual report to determine how the company reports its assets and worth (see example in Figure 4.3), or a task students of accountancy might be expected to perform during their studies. Harding (2007) offers some useful advice in this regard:

- Use contexts, texts and situations from the students' subject area. Whether they are real or simulated, they will naturally involve the language the students need.
- Exploit authentic materials that students use in their specialism or vocation – and don't be put off by the fact that it may not look like 'normal English'.
- Make the tasks authentic as well as the texts. Get the students doing things with the material that they actually need to do in their work. (Harding, 2007, pp. 10–11)

Authentic texts play an important role in demonstrating 'real' language use. If we aim to demonstrate to our class of nursing students the forms and features of nursing care plans, we would generally wish to show the class samples of authentic care plans. However, finding suitable authentic texts is not always easy. In discussing materials development in EAP, Swales (2009) describes a problem that can arise:

Most EAP practitioners, when preparing materials for classes or workshops, are probably familiar with that increasingly desperate feeling of, I can't find the perfect text for what I want to do in class. Hours, perhaps, of leafing through textbooks, manuals, journal articles or websites have failed to produce a solution to the material writer's problem. One text may have the looked-for rhetorical structure and linguistic exemplification, but the content is too obscure or unmanageable; another has attractive and utilizable content, but the structure is wrong, or the treatment is too journalistic (Myers, 1990), and a third looks promising but it is too cluttered with intertextual links, asides and references to be useable 'as is'. In addition, there is the question of whether the target audience will find the sample material sufficiently interesting to enable their attention to become appropriately focused on it, an issue that arises with texts that are more than a paragraph or so in length. Editing is, of course, always an option as is a certain amount of 'skeletonization', whereby ellipsis or some other 'place-holder' device is used to eliminate dense content chunks so that students can properly concentrate on rhetoric and language. Hence the EAP practitioner's dilemma: to keep on looking; to start editing; or to go somewhere else. (p. 5)

In response to this problem, Swales makes a case for the occasional use of 'instructor-written' materials and provides two suggestions for how these materials can be developed. The first suggestion is for the materials writer to create texts. Swales reports working with an EAP class for doctoral level students from mixed disciplines. The instruction focused on how to organize a set of abstracts from research articles and write up a literature review based on them. This called for a set of abstracts to be used as examples. Despite extensive searching the materials writers could not find suitable texts to use as is or that could be adapted and thus they devised their own. The second suggestion was to create an imaginary student's response to the materials. The materials writers had wanted to demonstrate how a literature review goes through several drafts before emerging in its final form. They wished to show why and how changes had been made across versions of a literature review. The materials writers examined many draft literature reviews they had obtained through teaching dissertation writing classes but to no avail. Therefore, they devised an imaginary character, Joyce, and created sections from her successive draft literature reviews and a narrative account of her responses to the information and texts she came across in writing. For example, the materials included a section from Joyce's first draft, with questions on this draft including *How is the literature in this first draft organized? Has Joyce included any evaluation of the previous literature?* The materials also noted feedback from her supervisor that this section was 'flat and boring' (p. 10).

The suggestions reported above highlight an important issue concerning the use of authentic texts. Although authentic texts are generally the preferred option in ESP, they can sometimes be too complex, either linguistically or in terms of content. Although we may wish to use authentic texts, if the information in them is beyond the understanding of our students, this will inevitably make for frustration and hinder the effectiveness of the instruction. Such cases may lead teachers and course developers to edit or adapt authentic texts or, as we have seen above, create ones of their own.

4.4 Evaluating courses and materials

Curriculum development involves planning a course at the outset but it also involves ongoing course revision. In deciding whether to revise a course, the developer first needs to know how effective the present version of the course is. One key source of information is student course evaluation. Teachers in many contexts around the world will be familiar with the kinds of during or end-of-course evaluations that are used, often questionnaires or interviews eliciting end users', students' and sometimes teachers' perceptions of the effectiveness of the course.

Perceptions of effectiveness are part of the picture. The other part is students' response to the course and learning from it. The course developer needs to consider *did the students like the course* and *did they learn anything from it?* The subject of evaluation has been relatively lacking in the ESP literature (Gillet and Wray, 2006; Cheng, 2006). Gillet and Wray argue that there has been little discussion of *success* in EAP, specifically the extent to which EAP programmes actually help their students to succeed in their chosen fields. These writers argue there is a need to 'fill the gap by looking at research that has attempted to provide evidence that EAP courses are helpful' (p. 8).

How then can we evaluate ESP and EAP courses and learning in them? Given that ESP courses aim to help learners with the demands of their target workplaces, professions or academic disciplines, what sets course evaluation in ESP apart from course evaluation in general is its focus on evaluating perceptions of effectiveness and assessing learning not only at the end of the ESP course but also in the light of subsequent experiences in the target field.

A number of interesting ideas for evaluating EAP courses can be found in the reports in the volume edited by Wray and Gillet (2006). The following examples from this volume were concerned with evaluating pre-sessional EAP courses and programmes in university settings. Atherton (2006) reports using mixed methods which included comparing students' entry and exit test scores, an end-of-course questionnaire which asked students to rate how well they felt they had achieved the main course objectives and the 'acid test' to find out how students felt they performed once they had joined their academic programmes. The 'acid test' took the form of a questionnaire sent to the students some months after they had finished the EAP programme and it included items such as:

> *I think the program enabled me to start my course with confidence;*
> *I feel I can cope with my studies;*
> *I was well informed about life at the university;*
> *I know where to get help if necessary.*
>
> (p. 17)

Ridley (2006) tracked students who after taking a pre-sessional course were completing their academic courses. The aim was to see if there was a relationship between the students' exit scores on the pre-sessional course and the time they took to complete their subsequent academic courses. Martala (2006) used both questionnaires and samples of students' writing to evaluate how well the writing component of a pre-sessional EAP programme equipped Chinese students for postgraduate studies in their chosen disciplines. A set of five questionnaires was used. The first questionnaire was given at the outset of the writing course and it aimed to gauge students' previous experiences of writing and writing instruction. Questionnaires 2, 3 and 4 were given at the end of each month of study on the course to gauge students' perceptions of what they were learning. The final questionnaire asked students to rate the course in light of their experiences as a postgraduate degree student. The evaluation also involved analysis of written assignments from the students while they were on the pre-sessional programme and while they were in the first semester of their degree programmes.

As argued earlier, students' perceptions are half the picture when it comes to evaluating the effectiveness of the courses and materials we have developed. We are also interested in whether students learnt what we had hoped they would. The remainder of this section discusses two studies focused on assessing learning in EAP contexts.

The first study focused on assessing learning of a written genre. Although only some EAP courses are entirely genre-based, many focus at least in part on genres. Yet discussion of learning in this kind of instruction has been limited. Cheng (2006):

> It seems that the ESP approach to writing instruction, as some genre-based theorists have noted (e.g. Johns, 2002), still remains an approach which privileges the analysis of learners' target genre needs and the preparation of teaching materials but has relatively little to say about actual learning by the learners who are consigned to such an approach. (p. 77)

Abbuhl (2005) reports a study offering support for genre-based instruction and feedback. The study was motivated by interest in the question of whether non-native speakers attempting to acquire discipline-specific genres are better served by being placed in content classes in which the conventions of the discourse community can be acquired intuitively through reading, lectures, interactions with lecturers and writing practice or from special instruction geared to help these L2 learners gain awareness of discipline-specific conventions of the target genres. The study investigated the relationship between teacher feedback and improvements in the quality of writing by students. Participants in the study were advanced ESL learners studying law at a US university. The study focused on learning of one particular legal genre, the office legal memorandum. (One of the law courses required students to write two drafts of this genre, a genre commonly used in legal settings.)

The writing of two groups of students was compared. The first group were students who volunteered to attend the English for Lawyers class. Over the course of a semester, students in this group received individualized feedback on the form (grammar and lexis) and content (legal argumentation and structural components) of their writing of memoranda. The second group received only one set of comments on the quality of their writing. The findings showed that while both groups made improvements in their writing, the feedback and instruction provided to the first group allowed them to make greater gains in organization and argumentation as well as in linguistic accuracy and the complexity of writing of this genre. Abbuhl notes that the extra feedback and instruction the first group received appeared to give them a 'greater awareness of their audience and of the genre-specific conventions of the US legal discourse community' (p. iv).

A second study (Crandall and Basturkmen, 2004) attempted to gauge learner response to and learning from a set of materials Crandall (1999) had developed to teach EAP students the speech act of requests in academic settings. Authentic samples of students' requests to lecturers during office hours were recorded and used as the basis for the development of a set of instructional materials. The materials required students to make close observations of segments from transcripts of authentic speaking and to participate in class discussions of pragmatic norms of requesting in academic settings. In order to assess the learning of students, a questionnaire was developed to assess their perceptions of the appropriacy of requests in a set of scenarios in academic contexts. (The scenarios and 'appropriate requests' were based on observations of the interaction between students and lecturers during office hours made in the earlier part of the study.) The EAP students completed the questionnaire before and after use of the instructional materials in class. Native speaker students also completed the questionnaire and their responses were used as a baseline against which the EAP students' responses were compared. The study found that the EAP students' responses were closer to those of the native speakers after the use of the materials and concluded that the students had indeed learnt something from the materials.

In recent years the topic of evaluation of materials in ESP has attracted the attention of researchers. A number of possible topics are evident in this area. Henry (2007) and Chan (2009) report studies evaluating very different topics. Henry investigated the effectiveness of using web-based materials in presenting a professional genre, the job application letter, to students of engineering and the students' response to this form of instruction. The study found that the students made significant gains in learning the genre and that they positively evaluated the instruction. Chan proposes a framework drawing on findings in discourse analysis and pedagogical considerations to evaluate ESP materials. Chan uses the framework to survey the units on 'meetings' in a number of published Business English textbooks.

4.5 Summary

Four areas of curriculum development have been discussed in this chapter – focusing the course, determining course content, developing materials and evaluating courses and materials. The discussion centred on the kinds of decisions that set the work of ESP course development apart from general language course development. The chapter has argued that there is no ready formula for determining ESP curricula; rather there are issues to be considered in each area of curriculum development.

4.6   Discussion

1. Investigate an ESP/EAP course offered in an institution in your own context. Where would you place it on the wide- and narrow-angled continuum? To help you decide, consider how the course is named and introduced in the 'statement of aims' and other introductory matter.
2. Now examine the syllabus from the course you examined in Question 1 above. How is the syllabus organized and what kinds of units of instruction does it involve (genres, skills, grammar and vocabulary, mixed)?
3. In relation to the course you examined in Questions 1 and 2, find out why it was designed as it was. Plan questions to use in an interview with the course developers. The interview will focus on the decisions they made about focusing the course and designing the syllabus. Why did they make the decisions they did? If possible, talk to the course developer and report your findings to the class or invite the course developer to the class for a question-answer session.
4. Think of an ESP course you currently teach or may teach in the future. What is the name of the course and what is its focus? Who are the students and what are some of their needs? Plan one unit of material for the course. You do not need to actually develop the materials. In your planning, consider the following items:

   What is the 'real content' of your material?
   Does it involve carrier content?
   What authentic texts will you use? Do you think suitable texts will be easy to find and would you consider other options suggested in 4.3?
   How could you evaluate learner response to or learning from the materials?

Part II
Case Studies in ESP Course Development

5
English for the Police

General descriptions of curriculum development in the literature may not show how courses are developed in response to a given situation and in light of the particular characteristics of the learners. The present chapter aims to show just that. The course was developed against a backdrop of real-world constraints, with course participants who were busy professionals (or professionals in training) and for whom learning about language and communication was only one of the things they had to contend with. The course in question was the English for Police course developed by Languages International, Auckland, for new police r+ing police-specific discourse presented a challenging task since they were also learning the language in general.

This chapter is organized into five sections. The first section describes the context of the course. The second and third sections describe how the course developers (who were also the teachers of the course) went about investigating learner needs and specialist discourse respectively. Realizing that the potential participants had a number of competing demands on their time and that they worked or studied on conflicting schedules, the course developers responded by devising a course around a set of web-based materials and a flexible course structure. The fourth section describes the course, the materials (a number of illustrations of the materials are given) and the evaluative process. The final section describes the particular difficulties and constraints presented by this case and how the course developers responded to them.

5.1 Context

The beginnings of the course development can be traced to the publication of an article in a local newspaper. The article featured a young man (Yuichi) who was hoping to become New Zealand's first ethnically Japanese policeman. However, as reported in the article, this aspiring policeman faced two hurdles, the language proficiency test and the fitness assessment. The article reported that Yuichi, having moved to New Zealand seven years previously, refused to give up his quest to become Auckland's first Japanese police officer. He had failed an English test the previous year but was told he would have a chance of acceptance if he could work on his language skills and fitness level.

Yuichi appeared to have ideas about how to work on the fitness problem but was less certain about how he could address the language problem. Reading this article, the Chief Executive Officer of the language school contacted the police force and set in motion a series of events leading to the development of the English for Police course. Initially the school had expected to offer the course for a small group of aspiring police personnel from a mix of first-language backgrounds including Mandarin, Japanese, Hindi, Persian, Korean and Cantonese. However, the course developers soon came to realize that there were potentially many more participants, due in part to the push within the police force for ethnic diversity and recruitment of more members from the Asian and Pacifica communities. The potential course members were expected to be in the main recruits on the Pre-College Employment Programme (PRECEP), a programme providing work experience before Police College, such as helping out on the public counter in police stations. This work was designed in part to enable recruits to upskill in various areas including literacy and communications. The language school originally anticipated that the course participants would spend one day a week at the language school.

However, ongoing consultations with the police organization revealed the potential for further and more varied course participants. A report written in the initial stages of consultation stated:

> The overall picture that emerged from consultation is of an organisation that has necessarily high standards in terms of workplace literacy but readily acknowledges that there are currently groups within the workforce who need more support. There is also an acceptance that the combination of a push for ethnic diversity in the workforce so that it more accurately reflects the ethnic make-up of the community and for the planned massive increases in the number of officers in uniform will increase the workplace literacy training needs of the organisation. The organisation is broadly supportive of any initiatives that will help its workforce communicate more effectively.

5.2 Investigating needs

Multiple sources of information

The course developers set about investigating needs through meetings with the police (notably those involved in recruitment and training) and visiting key sites such as the Police College and the Central Police Station in the city. On a visit to the Police College they were able to observe a writing class and sessions in which recruits gave presentations as part of their regular training. They were also able to analyse written texts supplied by the police and to talk to some of the sergeants who directly supervise the training of officers at the college. The course developers also went on 'ride-alongs' (car-based-patrol), often at night, with recently qualified ex-PRECEP members. Additionally, they carried out an assessment of the language proficiency of 14 potential participants (English as an Additional Language (EAL) members of PRECEP programme) using standardized and self-assessment instruments. They also conducted individual pilot assessments of these potential participants. Furthermore, police officers came to the course developers to explain the language problems or needs as they saw them and they also sent in many examples of written police work texts.

From these multiple sources of information, the course developers found that potential participants had advanced to higher levels of spoken English with some control of advanced idiomatic language, but faced particular problems in pronunciation, especially when speaking under pressure. Their proficiency in writing was found to be lower than their proficiency in speaking and there was some evidence of difficulties with collocations and connotations (vocabulary) and selecting an appropriate register or style for the types of writing required.

The course developers were aware that further needs analysis would be needed to provide a fuller picture, and the report from the initial needs analysis described above identified three areas still to be investigated which included speaking situations – exchanges between police officers, exchanges between police officers and members of the public and giving evidence in court. A more detailed second needs analysis was conducted one year after the initial needs analysis. In light of the findings from this second needs analysis and the course developers' increasing understanding of the situation derived from their ongoing contact with the police, three distinct sets of needs were identified (see Figure 5.1). These were needs related to the language that police use 'on the job', needs related to the language the recruits require to 'get through Police College' and needs related to further academic and/or specialist training. An example of the latter is language needed for 'legal 114', the university law course the officers take during the two years they spend as probationary constables after graduating from Police College. This course requires advanced academic language skills. During this probationary period, the officers often select a specialist area (such as crime, traffic police and frontline policing). Each specialist area presents particular language-based demands. Figure 5.2 shows a description of the language needs written by the course developers. The description details police recruits' 'on the job' language needs and highlights how these are different from their academic language needs.

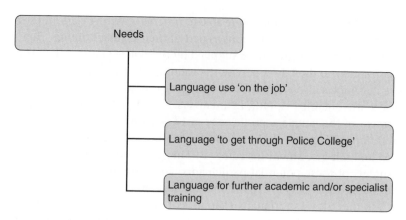

Figure 5.1 Types of needs in policing

Police-Specific Language:

Frontline officers need precise command of a range of language specific to the police. They use this language to talk about crimes, including suspect descriptions, locations, directions, crime scenes, description of vehicles, injuries, damage and police technical terms with colleagues, with the general public and with offenders. They need to use language accurately to avoid ambiguity with their colleagues, on the radio talking to Communication centres and to stand up to the scrutiny of defence lawyers in court. Much of frontline police work involves listening and speaking at high speed in stressful situations. Much of the work at the station requires high levels of sophistication in terms of writing clearly and accurately for a range of different audiences. Police officers must also be able to read quickly and effectively in order to make extremely important decisions which affect the lives of members of the public.

Academic Language

There is a discrepancy between the language demands of the job as a frontline officer and the more academic skills (listening to lectures/understanding texts/writing exam answers) needed to fulfil Police College requirements and successfully complete the compulsory university Law papers (post college). Some officers need support with this academic language both at college and after leaving. This discrepancy between frontline officers' language for work in the districts and academic language needed for study recurs at each promotional stage. In order to take sergeant's papers, officers need to go to college and to do more academic study. For some officers this can be a barrier to promotion.

Figure 5.2 Describing 'on the job' and academic language needs

5.3   Investigating specialist discourse

Alongside needs analysis

In this case, the investigation of specialist discourse was not a separate stage of course development but it proceeded hand in hand with the analysis of needs. This is illustrated below with reference firstly to the investigation of written discourse and secondly to spoken discourse.

In one 'needs analysis' interview with a senior police officer involved in training, the course developers enquired about the sorts of language and communication problems of student police officers. In response, the officer reported problems in the junior officers' writing of 'summaries of facts' that accompany 'interview summaries', two elements in the 'prosecution file' along with other reports such as the 'victim report'. Often the writing was too vague and had omissions. The course developers thus learnt that one incident requiring police intervention typically led to a series of written genres (reports). Report writing, it seemed, constituted a major part of a police officer's workload.

While discussing the elements in the 'prosecution file', the senior police officer provided sample reports. The course developers used these samples to elicit from the officer expectations for the various genres in question, including expectations of the schematic structure of reports (the type of content to be included and how it should be organized) and expectations for features of language use (such as preferences for the use of first person or third person pronouns). Discussion of the functions of the various reports with the senior police officer enabled the course developers to understand the criteria by which the reports were judged. They found out that the reports in the prosecution file needed to be very accurate and specific since the trial could be held months or years later when events would be hard to recall. Indeed, they discovered that it was precisely in these areas that new police officers struggled (often using vague language and insufficient detail in their reporting) to the extent that the senior police officer reported that he could not follow the series of events and the facts involved. A key feature of such reporting is the use of narrative accounts. The course developers also found out that there was an expectation that some reports such as the interview summary would be written in a more 'oral' style to reflect the fact that it was based on spoken evidence – 'it has to reflect what the witness is saying but it has to be written'. Not surprisingly, reporting interviews was a type of writing in which few new police officers were experienced.

The course developers also investigated spoken discourse. They were able to use the opportunities presented by the 'ride-alongs' to observe the language and speaking skills the officers used to deal with people on the streets. They have supplemented this information with observations of language use from watching the police television programmes (currently very popular in the local context) in which television cameramen follow police officers on patrol. The course developers are also looking into the possibility of obtaining transcripts of trials which they would use to observe how police officers present evidence in court. Additionally they are looking into the possibility of obtaining a corpus of police-spoken data developed overseas.

Privacy issues mean that there have been some restrictions on opportunities to 'observe' how the police used language in spoken interactions. One key spoken event that the needs analysis had revealed as potentially problematic was interviews. The course developers were not able to observe actual police interviews. However, one training officer provided 'tutorials' in the form of mock interviews to demonstrate to the course developers police expectations for interviewing. This was described as demonstrating 'how to conduct a decent interview'. The office both explained and demonstrated to the course developers the new principles that had recently come into practice and the techniques (termed 'investigative interviewing techniques') entailed. The new techniques involved the use of open questions to give the interviewee time to remember, to let the interviewee speak and to provide the interviewer space to plan the next step in the interview with the overall objective of not putting words into interviewees' mouths and contaminating witness reports (a key consideration in evidence to be presented in court).

5.4   Designing the course and materials

Flexible and individualized

The course originally developed primarily targeted PRECEP officers and the needs of the first category shown in Figure 5.1 (that is, language use 'on the job'). The course was developed with time constraints in mind: Not only would the course participants have very little time for language studies but they would also have to fit their language learning into busy schedules which might include night shifts. This meant that the course structure would need to be flexible and this requirement led to the development of a set of self-access, online lessons.

The results of the investigations of needs and specialist discourse were incorporated into the design of the course through the specification of course objectives. The objectives targeted language skills (writing and speaking), language knowledge (grammar and vocabulary) and language learner development (see Figure 5.3).

To develop students' writing skills in the context of:
    Police reports
    Statements of facts
    Job sheets
    Witness/victim/offender statements
    Victim impact statements
    Brief of evidence
    Note taking

To develop students' speaking skills in the context of:
    Interviewing
    Questioning

To develop students' awareness of vocabulary issues (specifically collocation, connotation and register) where relevant to police work.

To develop grammatical range and accuracy for both speaking and writing.

To foster learner autonomy by developing explicit knowledge of language, strategies for effective language learning and knowledge of available language learning resources both in and outside school.

Figure 5.3   Course objectives from the English for Police course

The results were also incorporated through the development of a police language corpus and the materials for self-access lessons which were to be used in conjunction with the corpus. This corpus comprises written texts largely supplied by the police during the needs analysis stage and also texts selected by the course developers from the police website. (It is envisaged that spoken texts will be added at a later point.) The self-access lessons contain tasks that require participants to conduct searches of the corpus and make observations of language use in it. These tasks focus on aspects of language that have been identified as language needs or difficulties. Materials for each lesson were reviewed and revised extensively. Having designed the materials, the teacher/course developer asked others at the Language school to review the materials: firstly the second teacher/course developer and then a pool of senior teachers. Feedback from others usually led to substantial revision. Once revised the material was trialled with the learners and then re-edited and modified.

Segments from one of the self-access, online lessons are shown in Figure 5.4. This lesson focuses on language for describing suspects. The segments are concerned with describing hair and build and the order of elements in a description. As can be seen, Task 5, Learning Point 3 and the Strategy Focus require the participants to make use of the Police Corpus. Other parts of this lesson (not shown in Figure 5.4) focus on additional elements of a description, such as age. The materials include a number of photographs of individuals and CCTV footage. (These visual elements are not shown in Figure 5.4.) A follow-on activity provided towards the end of this lesson refers participants to popular sports magazines and women's magazines in the School's Learning Centre. The activity suggests using the pictures in these magazines for extra practice in the language of description.

Initially, the course structure involved two modes of delivery – self-access, online lessons and one-on-one tutorials. However, feedback from the course participants showed a strong desire for a social form of learning, specifically, the participants clearly indicated they wanted a teacher and a class set-up. Consequently a third mode of delivery (a weekly class) was added to the course structure. Figure 5.5 shows the revised course structure for the PRECEP officers.

Materials developed for the group classes allow for teacher-led discussion and pair and group work. Figure 5.6 illustrates material for a group lesson, the Service Station Credit Card Case. This lesson focuses on interview planning and investigative interviewing techniques. It also involves a focus on language (cohesion) in the writing a summary of facts (type of written report).

In the eyes of the course developers, the most distinctive feature of the programme is the one-on-one tutorial provided to course participants on a weekly basis. These tutorials are used to provide personalized teaching for the officers' individual needs. In the tutorials the participants talk about their language studies over the previous week and any language issues arising in their work.

English for Special Purposes

Police work

Lesson		7: Language for suspect descriptions
Language		
✓	Text organization	Order of suspected descriptions
	Grammar	
✓	Vocabulary	Words used to describe ethnicity, build, hair, clothing, tattoos etc.
	Pronunciation	
Skills		
✓	Reading	Suspect descriptions (from job sheets, statements and NZ Police website)
	Writing	
	Listening	
✓	Speaking	Practice giving a spoken description

Strategy focus – notice the difference

A great language learning strategy is to be able to notice the difference between the words you use and the words other speakers use. When you have seen there is a difference, you can ask yourself questions like this:

- Which way is clearer? Why?
- The word X is new to me. What does it mean? Is it a word I can use?
- The word X is used with different grammar. Is there a difference in meaning?

If you can't answer the question yourself, write it down and bring it to your next tutorial.

You can practice this strategy with your answers to **Task 1** and the written descriptions in **Task 2**. Compare the language.

Note down in the boxes …

Words that are new to you.	Differences in the way you have used words.	Differences in the order of your description and the written descriptions.	Different ways of giving information.
Write here	Write here	Write here	Write here

Learning point 1: Order of descriptions

Descriptions of people all cover the following areas:

- ethnicity
- clothes waist down
- hair colour/length/style
- clothes waist up
- age
- height
- gender
- build
- other features – e.g. tattoos

The next task will help you work out the order of information in suspect descriptions.

Figure 5.4 Example of self-access, online lesson developed for the English for Police course

Task 3

Now read the 3 descriptions of suspects from the Police Corpus in the boxes. Look at the order of information in the descriptions and write a number in right column of the box. The first one has been done as an example.

Number

ethnicity

clothes waist down

hair colour/length/style

clothes waist up

age

height

gender

build

other features – e.g. tattoos

2.

Male Caucasian 5 foot 10 inches About 19 years old Lean but muscley build Blonde hair very short maybe a number two style cut Bright red hooded sweatshirt with cut off sleeves, with 'Players' across the chest in white writing Dark blue jeans scruffy looking torn at the bottom Wearing black shoes possibly boots Ethnic design tattoo on right lower arm
(source: Job Sheet)

1.

Male Caucasian
19 years old Long black hair to shoulder Slim Build Tattoo of tear drops on left cheek Black crew neck jersey Black jeans Dirty white sneakers
(source: Job Sheet)

3.

I would describe the male as a 35 year old Maori about 5'7" ft tall. He was of thin build. He had a moustache with black frizzy hair about shoulder length. His hair was tied in a ponytail. The offender was wearing a black leather jacket, which was quite fitting. He was wearing black jeans that were also tight and fitting. He was wearing black shoes.

I am not sure what he was wearing underneath the jacket but everything was black. He was scruffy looking. I did not notice any scars or tattoos.
(source: Statement)

In the real world ... descriptions all have the same order

Having a consistent order for descriptions in different types of police text is very useful. It means that:

- when you are interviewing, you remember to ask about all aspects of a suspect's description.
- when you are writing, again, you are less likely to forget important details.
- when you are reading and scanning a description for particular information you know where to look. For example, if you need to check whether an offender is Asian or Polynesian, you look at the beginning of the description.

In the real world ... Tattoos

Tattoos have very different meanings in different cultures.

- Read a music blog which talks about singer Amy Winehouse's teardrop tattoo
- Read about the history and tradition of Maori tattoos.
- Read an article from an art magazine called Log about prison tattoos in New Zealand.

Task 5

Now you will look at expressions you can use to describe different aspects of appearance. The following tasks involve using the NZ Police Corpus. If you are not familiar with how to use this Corpus, then do the police lesson called 'Using the NZ Police Corpus' first. Then come back to this lesson.

Look at these concordance lines below. Which word is missing?

Figure 5.4 Continued

1 about 30 years old; he had a slim build and blond	_ 1 now identify this person as the defend
2 Male Caucasian 19 years old Long black	_ to shoulder Slim Build Tattoo of tear drops on
3 t 19 years old Lean but muscley build No facial	_ Blonde hair very short, maybe a number two style
4 Driver.' Male Caucasian with dark, greying scruffy	_
5 Back seat passenger.' Female Maori with dark	_
6 25 years old * Slim build * Dark, short, thick	_ Clean shaven * Politely spoken Wearing baggy
7 Male Maori or Polynesian * 20 years old Bushy	_ * Wearing striped brown/grey shirt with white
8 early twenties * Short stocky stature * Facial	_ on his chin and upper lip *Long curly hair The
9 He had like a white singlet on, his	_ was greasy black & looked thick to about his ears
10 thin build. He had a moustache with black frizzy	_ about shoulder length His hair was tied in a pony tail
11 Asian in his 20's, large to fat build, short black	_ He was wearing a grey t-shirt, grey knee length
12 years, 5'1 0"– 6'O", slim build with short black	_ I said to them both for them to please not kick

Task 6

Look at the concordance lines in Task 5 again and complete the table below:

Learning point 3 – Describing hair colour

'**blond** or **blonde**'? There are two spellings for this word. Usually 'blond' is used for men and 'blonde' is used for women but as you can see from concordance lines 1 and 3 above, this is not always consistent.

'**brown**' – is not usually used in description of hair colour – but is used for the colour of a car. Try doing a search of the NZ Police Corpus for 'brown and hair' used together.

There are lots more words to describe hair in the NZ Police Corpus. Try your own search and add to the table above.

Strategy focus – Extend these tasks

When you are studying, you may decide that you need to go into more detailed research on a particular topic. For example, you may decide that you need more words to describe Caucasian hair. Here are some extension tasks that you can try:

1. There are lots more words to describe hair in the NZ Police Corpus. Try your own search and add to the table above.

2. Try a search in a General Corpus. See if any different words are used.

3. When you are at work and hear people giving descriptions, note down any different words they use and add them to your vocabulary notes.

Figure 5.4 Continued

The course runs for a 32-week period. It includes:

32 weeks of self-access learning and tutorial support (4 hours for the first 4 weeks/ 2.5 hours for the subsequent 4 weeks)

A weekly group lesson

Participants attend for one day per week as part of their programme.

Figure 5.5   Course structure in the English for Police course

Service station credit card case

This scenario is based on a true crime one of the teacher/course developers was involved in when working in another life as sales assistant in a petrol station.

There are 2 aims.

To develop pre-interview planning in order to get sufficient details from a witness interview and also to provide input on investigative interviewing techniques.

To practice adding cohesion to a written summary of facts

Procedure:

Before class: Give the scenario notes to a helpful teacher and explain the following:

You work as a sales assistant in a service station.

You called the police.

2 officers will come and interview you. This will happen in 2 stages – an initial interview (5 minutes) and a follow up interview which will be more detailed.

All the information you can remember is on the sheet. Anything else – you've forgotten.

Don't offer any extra information that you are not asked for.

In class:

Show picture of X Petrol Station on New North Road. Ask if anyone knows it? Where exactly it is? (Show map) Discuss the kinds of call outs you get to a petrol station.
Tell students they have been called out to attend an incident at the petrol station. You need to find: Atish Singh who called the Police.

Planning: Before you get to the scene, think about:

– how you will find Atish and introduce yourself
– what you will say to him to get a free recall (Note: this means to get the big picture so that you have a pretty clear idea of what happened/who was involved/what offence has been committed – you don't make detailed notes at this stage and you don't need precise details. For this you should be very general: What's happened here? would be a good start.

Free recall: Find the service station attendant. Get the big picture. (Note you should watch what they say and then give feedback on manner/whether they sound in control/professional/ the way they greet the person/whether they put Atish at ease/whether they explain the process ... e.g. free recall then detailed questions).

Back to the classroom. Feedback on performance so far...

e.g. Do you have a fairly clear idea of what's happened here?

Now plan ... what details should you find out now:

Complainant's details (full name/home address/date of birth/home phone/cell phone//work address/work phone)

Figure 5.6   Service station credit card case lesson

Times/dates

Other witnesses/workers/customers

Description of suspect (ethnicity/gender/age/height/build/distinguishing features/hair/tattoos/jewelery/top/trousers/shoes)

Description of vehicle he left in

Actions – what he did/what shop assistant did. chronological order & what was said. Precise movements around the service station

Exhibits – contaminated?

CCTV: Decide who is going to ask for what.

Go back to witness and carry out a detailed interview.

Make notes on notebook template.

Back in the classroom debrief.

Use TEDS (Tell me/Explain how/Describe/Show me)

Use diagrams (e.g. of the forecourt/the shop with location of counter/oils/cigarettes/office/cameras)

Enough details?

Read the summary of facts text and spot any details that you missed.

Improve the cohesion of the Summary of Facts report by adding cohesive devices in the gaps.

Information for witness:

You are Atish Singh
d.o.b. 25.05.1990
address: Unit 14b / 3 Woodward Road
hm phone: 8154387
mob: 02128985734
Occ: part time sales assistant (Xco Service Station 1060 New North Road)
wk phone 8152273 x 3

When the officers come for the first time (750pm) you say only the following things:

This man tried to buy a lot of stuff here. I thought it was a bit suspicious and checked out the card. It turned out to be stolen. When I told the guy he did a runner and drove away. When the officers come back you can add the rest of these details (when asked) again – don't provide anything that you are not asked to provide.
7.25. (12 May 2009) man entered. car parked outside
you were alone in the shop (no customers, no other staff – manager had gone for a break) you were restocking the chewing gum shelf
man looked around shop for a couple of minutes.
no petrol.
you then went behind counter
he looked at oil
took 4 × 1 litre bottles of XTX to counter (from shelf)
you said 'how's your day going sir?'
he said 'I wanna buy some smokes.'
asked for 7 packets of cigarettes
wanted to pay with credit card (NBNZ VISA name ROBIN MASTERS)
suspicious (remembered Service Station memo about credit card fraud)
said: 'just need to check this card, sir. won't be a moment'
took card to office behind 1 way glass (could still see guy)
called visa gave details of card (guy looking around)
still no one in shop. no cars on forecourt
visa said 'cut card in front of customer. call 111'
you went back to counter. Said 'sorry sir this card is reported stolen.'
he said nothing but ran off
left cigs + oil on counter (he touched them / you haven't moved them)

Figure 5.6 Continued

got in car
drove away up Woodward
you called 111

Shop layout:

man – white male/tall/thin but broad shouldered/late 30s?/short dark hair – unshaven/maybe an earring – stud/no tattoos/black v neck wool jumper! white t underneath/dark trousers? jeans?/shoes????
Carwhite
ford falcon sedan
late model
Rego TV9262?

Petrol Station Lesson

1. What will you say to get a free recall?
2. What areas will you need details of? List them:
   e.g. time frame:
3. For each area: decide what details you need:
   e.g. Car: make/model/year/colour/rego/distinguishing features

Worksheet

SUMMARY OF FACTS

_____ 19:25 on the evening of 12 May 2009, the defendant in this matter, Arnold LOGAN, entered the Xco Service Station, 1060 New North Road.

_____, Atish SINGH, the complainant, was the only person working on the premises. He was restocking shelves when LOGAN walked in.

_____, LOGAN, looked around the shop. Meanwhile SINGH took up position behind the counter. After a couple of minutes, LOGAN took 4 × l litre bottles of XTX oil off the oil shelf and put them on the counter in order to purchase them.

_____ the defendant, SINGH asked if there was anything else LOGAN wanted. LOGAN said he wanted to 'buy some smokes.' He asked for 7 packets of cigarettes from behind the counter.

_____, SINGH placed the cigarettes on the counter in front of LOGAN.

_____ LOGAN produced a silver NBNZ Credit card with the name 'ROBIN MASTERS' on it. His suspicions aroused and remembering a recent memo from BP about people buying high value shop goods with credit cards, SINGH took the card to the office and called VISA.

_____ SINGH was instructed to destroy it in front of the customer and call 111.

_____ SINGH returned to the counter and informed LOGAN that the card was reported stolen and that he would need to cut it up.

At this point, LOGAN left the shop in a hurry, got into a vehicle parked on the forecourt and drove off up Woodward Road towards the city.

_____ the car's registration details, SINGH dialed 111 and reported the incident.

Constables Deng and Cheong from Avondale Police attended the _____ , took the witness's statement and _____ the following exhibits: discs of CCTV footage from the shop cameras; the bottles of oil; the packets of cigarettes; the credit card.

At approximately 20.00 hours, on the same evening, LOGAN was stopped on Great North Road, near the junction with Chevalier Road by Constable JONES, QID 1845 from Henderson Police, who had been told by Communications to look out for a vehicle matching the description of the car SINGH had provided,

_____, LOGAN was arrested and taken to Avondale Police Station. He was questioned and admitted trying to use a stolen credit card. _____ his finger prints were later found to match those found on the bottles of oil.

He was _____ charged with attempting to use a stolen credit card.

LOGAN is a 39 year old male who has not previously appeared in court.

Figure 5.6 Continued

They might, for example, report on any self-access lessons they have worked on and receive feedback on the writing they have done in these lessons or feedback they have received from their supervisors at work (for example, feedback on the police reports they have written). The tutorials are used for individualized instruction. For instance, one recruit who had recently started working in a domestic violence unit needed to work on vocabulary of violence and needed to know the precise differences in connotation between words such as 'slap' and 'punch'. The tutorials are also used to plan the following week's work. For example, the tutor and the recruit who had recently started working in the domestic violence unit planned searches for the recruit to make using the corpus (such as a search to identify collocations for 'argue' and 'argument'). A key feature of the tutorials is the focus on learner training. As far as possible the tutors try to elicit the solutions for the problems from the participants themselves. The aim is for the participants to become more independent in their learning and better able to identify and exploit potential language resources.

Evaluation process

To evaluate the course and learning of individual participants, the course developers track participants' progress through internal and external measures. Internal assessment involves the use of proficiency and competency language tests and comparison of scores with initial assessments. External assessment involves working with the police to identify improvements in the participants' ability to cope with the language demands of Police College and to see if they develop acceptable levels of language for policing. Feedback from key stakeholders (such as, staff at Police College, police workplace assessors, the participants' colleagues and supervisors, police recruitment managers and the course participants) plays a major role in this process. Key questions for this feedback are whether the course participants are performing more effectively in their workplace assessments, gaining better feedback from their workplace assessors on their language and communication skills and whether their language and communication skills have developed sufficiently enough for them to go through to Police College.

5.5 Responding to difficulties and constraints

As has been mentioned above, there were some constraints on obtaining authentic spoken texts for the analysis of needs and specialist discourse. These constraints were due to the confidential nature of police spoken exchanges with suspects and members of the public. Creative solutions were devised by the course developers and included their use of television programmes, recording police on patrol and at work and the police in providing 'mock' interviews.

One difficulty in developing this course arose from the individual nature of the needs of the course participants. The course developers responded by developing self-access lessons (in which course participants select lessons to work on) and the one-on-one tutorial system (see section 5.4). Needs also varied across the group of course participants and three different types of needs were identified (see Figure 5.1). To try to 'cover' these different types of needs in the one programme would have been unrealistic, and given the preponderance of PRECEP officers on the course, the course developers decided to focus the initial programme on needs in the first category (language use on the job) to meet the participants' 'immediate' needs as opposed to their longer-term needs.

For the course developers themselves, the development of the course entailed a steep learning curve since they had no direct experience of working in the police. They were able, however, to obtain 'insider' information through the help provided by individual senior police officers. Of particular importance were the insights these officers have provided regarding the functions, expectations and values of the police community for the various genres in their work (for example, the functions of the various reports, the criteria by which they are evaluated, the conventional sequencing of content and linguistic expression). Although some limited literature on police discourse is available, it is largely based on analysis of data collected in other countries. Thus the course developers obtained the bulk of their information from their own empirical observations of texts – in other words, their description and understanding was developed from scratch and in this they drew in part on approaches to language description to which they had been introduced in teacher education courses.

5.6 Summary

This chapter reported the development of the English for Police course, a course originally triggered by a chance reading of a newspaper article. In devising the course, the course developers have come to learn a lot about police work. In interviewing the course developers I remarked that now they probably knew enough to join the police themselves. (One of them responded saying that this may have been the case but they wouldn't have passed the fitness test!)

Despite limitations on the course developers' knowledge of policing before embarking on this project, the course that has emerged is very much focused on police language use 'on the job' – the forms and features of communication in police reports, interviews and everyday spoken exchanges. The chapter has described the 'investigative work' the course developers have done in order to produce descriptions of 'on the job' language use. This work involved talking to senior officers about the language needs of junior officers and the police community's expectations for the genres through which policing is done (the various types of reports and interviews and the everyday spoken exchanges). It has also involved the collection and analysis of samples of these genres.

5.7 Discussion

1. How would you classify the English for Police Course in relation to the categorizations shown in Figure 1.1 (Areas of ESP Teaching) and Figure 1.2 (Time of Course in Relation to Experience)?
2. Where would you situate the English for Police course on the wide- and narrow-angled continuum discussed in Chapter 4?
3. Friedenberg et al. (2003) outline three questions for needs analysis in workplace language training:
   a. What functions and tasks does the employee need to do?
   b. What language competencies are required to perform these functions and tasks well?
   c. How does the employee currently do these functions?
   Select one of the 'on the job' police functions or tasks mentioned in this chapter and outline how you would investigate Questions b and c in relation to it.
4. The use of corpus-based searches of language has proved to be very popular with the police recruits. Police tend to enjoy 'investigative' type work and the corpus-based searches used as part of the teaching/learning methodology bears some resemblances to investigative methods used in policing. In this way, the course makes 'use of the methodology and the activities of the field it serves' (referred to in Chapter 1). In your opinion, how important is it for ESP course developers to consider links between language-teaching methodologies and the methods and activities used in the target discipline or profession?
5. One focus of the English for Police course is 'learner training', reflecting in part the course developers' beliefs in the value of fostering learner autonomy. Chapter 2 reviewed Hyland's (2008, p. 113) argument that needs analysis is not entirely objective and that, similar to other classroom practices, it involves decisions based on teachers' interests, values and beliefs about teaching, learning and language. What beliefs do you have in *one* of these areas (learning, teaching or language)? How might these beliefs impact on how you set about analysing needs?
6. What skills and areas of expertise did the course developers draw on in developing this course? How do you evaluate your present skills and expertise in these areas? Which of these skills and areas of knowledge do you think should be focused on in ESP teacher education and which are best acquired 'on the job' (while working as a teacher)?

Acknowledgement

I would like to thank Nick Moore and Peter Nicolls of Languages International, Auckland, for the generous use of their time and for providing access and information on the development of the course described in this chapter. I would also like to express my gratitude to the directors of Languages International and the New Zealand Police.

6
English for Medical Doctors

The present chapter describes an ESP course designed not only for a very specific group of learners but also for those learners' needs in one particular communicative event. This event had been highlighted as likely to be an area of particular difficulty for a number of the prospective learners on the course. The course was developed to help a group of overseas-trained medical doctors who were preparing to sit medical registration examinations in New Zealand. The communicative event in question was the patient-centred medical consultation.

The ESP literature has long since argued the need for course development to include investigation of the nature of discourse in events as practised in the particular professional, work or study context to which the learners are headed. The literature also suggests that the languag e descriptions provided by ESP courses should be *specific* to discourse in that context, rather than *generic*. However, just how course developers and teachers set about this investigation is not always self-evident in the literature. The present chapter shows how one course developer, who was also the teacher of the course, investigated discourse in doctor–patient interviews to provide a description that would inform her teaching of the course she modestly refers to as 'English Language' lessons.

In the local community it was important that doctor–patient interactions were patient-centred and consultative. The course developer set about investigating and analysing the nature of discourse in consultations as practised by highly regarded medical practitioners in the local context. Her aim in doing this was to provide a fine-grained description of the features of discourse expected in the community, a description that would underpin much of the instructional material that was subsequently developed for the course. Given that the ESP teacher was not a medical practitioner herself, her objective was to find out 'what patient-centred management was all about and how that translated into language'.

Like the previous chapter, the present chapter is organized into five sections. The first section offers a description of the context of the course. The second outlines the reasons why the patient-centred consultation was seen as an area of particular need. The third describes how the course developer investigated discourse in the consultations and the expectations held for these consultations in the local context. The fourth section describes the course and the materials along with illustrative samples. The fifth section describes the difficulties and constraints presented by this case and how the teacher/course developer resolved them.

6.1   Context

New Zealand receives thousands of new immigrants each year. Many immigrants apply on the basis of a skills and a points system in which applicants achieve points for areas such as educational background, English language proficiency and age. A number of immigrants are overseas-trained doctors who, if they who wish to work as medical doctors in New Zealand, are generally required to pass registration examinations set by the Medical Council.

In 2001 a medical 'bridging programme' was established by the Clinical Training Agency (a governmental organization) in conjunction with the two medical training universities in the country. The aim of the programme was to provide a course of study that would support a number of overseas-trained medical doctors in their preparations for the registration examinations. The bridging programme ran eight times over four years beginning in 2001, provided courses on medical topics such as gynaecology and psychology in addition to a course on professional development. The teacher/course developer who is the subject of this chapter taught the programme six times. The trainers on the professional development course were themselves general practitioners and psychotherapists who had trained and were practising in New Zealand. The course focused on medical ethics and communication skills, including communication in a key event, the patient-centred consultation. The doctors' performance in such consultations constituted one area of assessment in the registration examinations. The first time the bridging programme had been offered, the professional development course had not included English language instruction. However, the professional development trainers had noticed that a number of the overseas-trained doctors participating in the course had difficulties in conducting medical consultations and that their difficulties appeared to be at least in part related to English-language problems. The convenor of the professional development course requested the services of an ESP specialist (a teacher who had previous experience of teaching medical English in a different setting) to develop and teach a course of English Language instruction.

The focus of the present chapter is on the English course developed as part of the professional development course at the University of Auckland, one of the two medical training universities participating in the bridging programme. The English courses had 12–15 doctors in a class. The doctors came from a variety

The Professional Development Course

Introduction

Health care professionals require good communication, reflective and practical skills, and an understanding of the ethical and social dimensions of health care practice. This course has been designed to update your skills and understanding to the level required of doctors working in New Zealand.

The course will include up-skilling in the areas of doctor-patient relationship, communication skills, ethics, cultural sensitivity, medico-legal obligations, reflective practice and professional development. There will be a focus on the process within the consultation and using the patient-centred method.

The course is held one day a week. Each week there will be a workshop on a professional development topic and a further session on some aspect of communication skills. The afternoon will be divided into two sessions.

In one, you will practice consultation skills in small groups, using role play in simulated consultations. Actors will be involved in the consultations and in giving feedback. We will record consultations on video, so you can learn by watching yourself consulting.

*In the second, you will have the opportunity to learn the subtle English Language skills required in medical practice.

Figure 6.1 Introduction to the professional development course for overseas-trained medical doctors
Source: Adapted from Hawken, S. and Fox, R. (2004) *Professional Development Course Handbook.*

of countries and regions including South East Asia, the Middle East and Eastern Europe. They were all experienced. Some had worked in English-medium hospitals, although communication in these hospitals may have been more 'doctor-centred' as was the case in New Zealand. The doctors had a generally high proficiency in English since they needed an overall high English-language proficiency level to be accepted onto the bridging programme. Not all of the doctors would necessarily have had a particularly high score for speaking, however, and some of the doctors had near-native fluency in English. The first time the English course was offered, attendance was optional. However, a few of the doctors who would have benefitted most did not attend and so the second time the course was offered, attendance was made compulsory. Figure 6.1 shows part of the Introduction to the *Professional Development Course Handbook*. The introduction explains the aims the course and shows how the ESP course, the 'English Language lessons' (*), related to the aim of upskilling the doctors in the areas of patient-centred consultations and communication skills. As explained in the introduction, the purpose of the English lessons was to support the consultations by focusing on the 'subtle' use of language and language skills the consultations required.

6.2 Investigating needs

In this case, the doctors' area of greatest need had been specified before the ESP teacher came on board since the professional development trainers had noticed an area of communication (the patient-centred consultation) in which a number of the doctors in the first cohort of the bridging programme had experienced some language difficulties. Because of this observation, the trainers contacted the ESOL section within the university and asked for the services of an ESP teacher to design a course of instruction. Although the professional development trainers were able to identify an area of communicative need, they were not language specialists (they were medical practitioners or psychotherapists and they were not able to identify within this area the precise sources of the problem in terms of 'diagnosing' which aspects of language were important in patient-centred consultation and aspects of language use that the doctors did not yet have full control over). Identifying the source of the problem became the task of the ESP teacher along with providing appropriate instruction, the 'remedy'. As the ESP teacher explained, the professional development trainers said that the English of some of the doctors 'was not that good but they were quite vague about what exactly it was that was not good'.

The ESP teacher/course developer was given a short 'lead time' (time to prepare the course in advance of teaching it) of two weeks. This meant that the analysis of needs in terms of what exactly constituted the doctors' language difficulties in this event, proceeded as in the words of the teacher in a 'find out as you go' manner. She sat in on demonstration role plays that were provided in the sessions given by the professional development trainers and watched videotapes of the overseas doctors in role play medical consultations. Largely, the teacher investigated needs at the same time as she was teaching the 'lessons'.

Since it was the doctors' performance in the doctor–patient consultations that had been the impetus for 'English Language' lessons, it made sense to try to find out what language skills and language use these events seemed to require and what it was that the doctors could not do or did not know in relation to them. The teacher sat in on the role play medical consultation sessions held by the professional development trainers. The trainers were themselves highly experienced registered medical practitioners in New Zealand and were working partly in medical education as well. They were individuals whose interpersonal and patient management skills were highly regarded by their peers. In the sessions the doctors, who were organized into small groups, practised consultation skills through the use of role play in simulations. In these sessions the trainers modelled the doctor's role in doctor–patient consultations and also set up role plays between the overseas-registered doctors and actors. The actors played the role of the 'patients' with a variety of health problems. The trainers gave feedback to the 'doctors'. The actors also took part in giving feedback to the 'doctors' for example, by commenting on how clearly they understood the questions the doctors asked or the information they gave, or how they felt in response to how the doctors handled the interaction in the consultations.

The teacher's observations of the trainers' modelling of a patient-centred consultative style, the doctors' performance in the role plays and the feedback the

Establishes initial rapport; builds the relationship – develops rapport
Establishes patient's concern; understands the patient's perspective
Explores and clarifies from a medical perspective
Explores physical, social and psychological factors
Provides structure to the consultation; pacing, flow, logical sequence, closure
Offers and explains diagnosis; provides information, seeks shared understanding
Shares decision making; offers options to achieve a clear management plan
Sensitive to patient's views; checks back and encourages patient to contribute

Figure 6.2   Criteria in the Observed Consultation Appraisal Form

doctors received on the role plays provided a good deal of information about needs. She was able to find out what the medical community's expectations were for how doctors should manage this event. Her observations of the sessions gave her what she described as 'my first feeling for what patient-centred consultations were'. At a macro level she was able to see how the event was expected to be structured and sequenced and at a micro level she was able to identify the 'subtle' uses of language that were expected to be part of the doctors' linguistic repertoire, the expectations of the trainers for doctors' language use and the aspects of specialist language in patient-centred consultations which some of the doctors had limited awareness of.

In an attempt to understand the precise nature of expectations for the patient-centred interview, she also drew on information in a key document, The Observed Consultation Appraisal Form. The form, which is used in the registration examination, lists the criteria used to determine effective communication including *establishing rapport, understanding the patient's perspective* and *offering options*. The complete list of criteria is shown in Figure 6.2.

6.3   Investigating specialist discourse

As described above, what the ESP course should focus on in this case was clear from the beginning. Its focus was on needs in the area of patient-centred consultations, especially the doctors' use of 'subtle' English within these consultations. However, although there was general agreement that this was the area of need that the ESP course was to focus on, what was not known at the outset was precisely what constituted these 'subtle' language uses. This was an area of discourse that remained to be explored and the course developer's immediate objective was to investigate the nature of language use within consultations with the aim of providing a description of language use for pedagogy. The remainder of this section describes how the course developer examined language use in consultations, the features of discourse she identified as salient in this particular type of setting and the features which needed to be brought to the attention of at least some of the overseas-trained doctors who were not already aware of them or had not already incorporated them into their linguistic repertoire. The concern of the ESP teacher in this stage of course development was to address the question of what constitutes appropriate use of English in doctor talk in patient-centred consultations.

Multiple sources of information

The teacher made use of multiple sources of information to help her address this question. The sources included the following:

1. Observations of the role plays between the overseas-trained doctors and actor 'patients' and the feedback comments made by the professional development trainers on the doctors' performance and use of language in the role plays. In addition, each week the professional development trainers reported to the ESP teacher the communication and language problems they had noticed in the doctors' performance in the role plays that week. The teacher noted ways the language use of some of the overseas-trained doctors might be at variance with local norms (for example, the rather directive and abrupt 'I need to examine you now' rather than the softer form 'What needs to happen now is that I need to examine you').
2. Observations of authentic medical consultations in two general practice clinics in suburban settings. Arrangements for these observations were made by the ESP teacher together with the professional development trainers. The general practitioners had been selected as providing good models of patient-centred management style. The ESP teacher approached patients in the waiting room to explain the purpose of her study and to ask permission to sit in on their medical consultation. The purpose of the observations was to gather authentic samples of language use in doctor–patient consultations in the local context.

   The teacher found that the authentic medical consultations differed in one key respect from those portrayed in the role plays with the actors. Whereas the authentic consultations were characterized by a strong emotional and affective content, emotional content was generally missing in the role plays since everyone knew the situation was not for real. During the observations of medical consultations, the teacher made handwritten notes of what the doctor said and in some cases what the patient said, especially noting any less formal and idiomatic uses of language (for example, she noted a patient remarked 'these tablets seemed to *do the job*', an idiomatic way of saying the tablets were effective).

   Although extremely useful as a means of collecting samples of authentic discourse, the teacher's observations were nevertheless challenging to manage. It was important for the teacher as an observer not to intrude on what was the intimate doctor–patient relationship and to position herself physically as far as possible out of view. 'I hadn't realized the emotional and affective connection between a doctor and patient', she reported.

3. Filmed materials including a television series offering a 'fly on the wall' perspective of day-to-day interactions between doctors and patients. The series, filmed at a hospital in Australia, recorded authentic interactions between hospital specialists and patients over courses of diagnosis and treatment. The materials also included a video recorded at the university hospital in which the ESP course was run. This recording showed medical school staff conducting demonstration consultations with professional actors. Once more the teacher made notes on uses of language reflecting patient-centred management or idiomatic uses of language (for example, in making a transition and leading into a sensitive topic a doctor said, 'I'd like to ask you a question I ask all my patients. Do you smoke?').

The reader may at this point wonder why the course developer did not turn to published course books on topics such as English for Doctors or Medical English rather than conducting her own investigation into discourse in doctor–patient consultations. Would not such works provide a useful source of information on doctors' use of language and would they not contain some description of language use in medical consultations that could be used directly in teaching without the need for empirical study of discourse? Although the course developer examined a number of such published works, she found the examples of consultations unsuitable since even in the good-quality commercial texts, examples of doctor–patient discourse were generally simulated and thus more bland and straightforward than authentic discourse. The texts often aimed for a balance between authenticity and comprehensibility for teaching purposes and suppressed the subtlety of real interaction between doctors and patients and the kinds of distressed, fearful, confused and emotional states she observed in naturally occurring events.

Secondly, the very specific nature of the consultations required in the New Zealand context, the fact that the consultations needed to be patient-centred and consultative and that the doctors were expected to draw on local varieties of language use including idiomatic uses of language, precluded the adaptation of course book materials developed for an international or UK/US based population. Furthermore, the description of doctor–patient consultations these materials tended to provide was very limited and often portrayed a more doctor-centred approach that was incompatible with the values in the local context. Given the importance of developing the overseas-registered doctors' language skills in this particular event, it was clear that a more extensive level of detail and linguistic description was called for. The published course books covered a number of areas of doctor–patient communication and all four skill areas and clearly covered them in less detail than was required for the present course with its focus on the one specific event. The published course books generally targeted a wider audience than the present ESP course, often targeting medical students as well as qualified doctors and intermediate level learners of English. Because of this, the works tended to focus on introducing the audience to communication in medical consultations rather than upskilling the audience. Furthermore, the works were inclined to introduce language content that was pitched too low for the learners on the present course who were relatively advanced, and in some cases highly advanced learners.

Features of discourse in patient-centred medical consultations

The course developer derived a good deal of information about the content and organization of the consultations from the instructional materials developed by the professional development trainers. From this source, she found that the consultations were typically organized into four stages (initiating the consultation, gathering information, explaining and planning, and closing the session) and that each stage involved its own typical set of procedures. For example, the first stage, initiating the session, would include *greeting the patient* and introducing oneself as the doctor, clarifying the doctor's role, making a human connection (such as *You look worried* or *that's a nasty cough*), the initial question (such as *What brings you here today?)* and identifying the patient's main problem.

From her observations of language use in consultations in the general practice clinics, the role plays and feedback comments from the professional development trainers, the course developer identified a set of key features of the discourse in such consultations which at least some of the doctors found difficult. These included a number of pragmatic functions (such as *showing empathy, asking about symptoms, responding to patients' concerns* and *explaining a diagnosis*) and key lexical areas including idiomatic ways of *describing pain* and *naming symptoms*. Since the doctors managed the interaction, they needed to use *transitions* to signal the function of the upcoming discourse. They also needed to show responsiveness to what their patients said by using *feedback responses*. Furthermore, her observations showed that doctors had specific ways of introducing *particularly sensitive issues* (such as the patient's sexual history, drug or alcohol habits) into the conversation and revealed the critical role of *hedging* (softening) and tentativeness in doctor talk.

Some examples of language use drawn from the course developer's samples of observed language use are shown in Figure 6.3. The features and examples in this figure represent only a small fraction of those identified and recorded by the course developer. Figure 6.3 shows the features in isolation. The idiomatic expressions were common in New Zealand English but may be far less so elsewhere. Some features, such as idiomatic ways of naming symptoms, were features the doctors needed to be able to understand as well as produce since they were forms of expression used by patients.

Feature	Categories	Samples of language use
Key pragmatic functions	Showing empathy	*So you lost your husband six months ago and you're finding it hard to cope, physically and mentally. This must be a difficult time for you.*
	Asking about symptoms	*I'd just like to ask some questions if that's ok?* *Any other thing you're noticing nowadays?* *So how long have you been like this?* *Can you tell me a bit more about it?* *What brings it on?* *Can you tell me how long ago it started?*
	Responding to the patient's concerns	*I understand your concerns but I'd just like to ask a few more questions to understand the situation.* *It's the third time. That's quite a bit isn't it?*
Lexical fields	Idiomatic ways of describing pain	*a dragging pain, the odd pain, it comes and goes, shooting pains*
	Idiomatic ways of describing symptoms	*be under the weather, broke out in this red rash, it knocks it out of me, have a screw missing, have a bit of trouble going to the toilet (rather than I'm constipated)*
Discourse transitions		*What needs to happen now is an examination (rather than I now need to examine you).* *The next step now is to check you over.*
Eliciting feedback responses		*Does that sound sensible to you?* *Am I being clear in all this?* *How does this sound to you?*
Dealing with particularly sensitive issues		*Do you mind if I ask you ...?* *Do you think we can do something about your smoking?* *Do you ever think of cutting down on your drinking?* *I realize that this is difficult for you but if you could tell me a bit about ...* *I know a lot of people your age have ...*
Hedging		*I'd just like to talk about ...* *Do you mind if I ask you a few things that may not seem related ...*

Figure 6.3 Selection of salient discourse features and illustrative samples of language use

In reality, a number of such features are used in conjunction in speaking. The short excerpt below has been abridged from the ESP teacher's notes on an authentic exchange in a general practice clinic. It shows a mixture of features described above. In particular, this segment shows idiomatic and non-medical word choices, hedges and tentative uses of language, features that are used alongside each other. For example, in responding to the patient's remark about being 100 per cent happy the doctor uses the hedge *just*, the idiomatic expression *hit on the head* and the non-medical word choice *give you* (rather than prescribe). In this utterance, the doctor also says somewhat tentatively *I might just give you* (rather than *I will give you …*) which can be interpreted as an attempt to avoid an authoritarian and directive stance. Other idiomatic word choices in this excerpt are *clear up* and *out of the woods* (rather than *recovered*). The use of these features can be seen as appropriate language choices for 'patient-centred' communication. The non-medical and idiomatic word choices in preference to medical and formal words indicate an attempt to 'establish rapport' by using language similar to what a patient would use, a strategy to avoid putting a distance between the doctor and the patient. The tentative uses of language and hedging indicate an attempt to minimize asymmetrical power and knowledge relations in the interaction between doctor and patient, and an attempt to 'offer options' by making a suggestion rather than taking control through telling the patient what the doctor intends to do.

Excerpt 1

DOCTOR: How's the ear?
PATIENT: It's *cleared up* completely. It's popped and doing what it should.
DOCTOR: What was worrying me but I couldn't see it because the drum was behind. I can see your drum now. You're not *out of the woods* completely. It *just* needed that *little* extra time.
PATIENT: I'm 100% happy.
DOCTOR: The main thing is that the drum moves now. There still is debris and it's still inflamed. I *might just* give you an extra prescription *just* to *hit it on the head*. But clearly you've made good progress.

6.4 Designing the course and materials

For the ESP teacher in this case, the main consideration in designing the course was the specification of course content, that is, specification of what to teach. In Chapter 5 we saw that a good deal of consideration had to be given to how the course would be offered in terms of the mode of delivery, since the course participants in that case were working on varying shifts as well as studying. In the present case, the course participants were on a full-time course of study, the 'bridging course', and the 'English Language' lessons were scheduled to fit into the structure of one unit on that programme, the Professional Development unit, which was held on the Friday of each week for a duration of 14 weeks. The lessons lasted 90 minutes and ran concurrently with the role play sessions. Given that the overseas-trained doctors were senior professionals, the teacher considered it important not to run the course as 'lessons' – there were no desks and no requirements for the doctors to fill in any of the exercises (although many did). For the role play sessions, the doctors were split into small groups and each week two groups did a role play of a medical consultation with an actor as the 'patient' (the other doctors were the audience). The role plays were video recorded. The professional development trainers gave feedback to the doctors on their performance. The doctors were able to use the video recordings to observe and reflect on their own performance.

Although the impetus for the course had come from the professional development trainers, and although the teacher worked closely with the trainers, discussing the doctors' language needs and the design of the English-language course as a response to those needs on a weekly basis, it was nevertheless very much up to the ESP teacher to specify the nature of the English-language course. As she said:

> The professional development trainers told me what they had noticed about the doctors' communication difficulties. They saw these difficulties as language related but they couldn't be specific about what these difficulties were and they did not say what I should teach in the English course. It was really up to me to determine the parameters of the course.

The ESP course she devised was broadly structured around the sequence followed in Patient-Centred Consultations. This sequence is implicit in the 'Observed Consultation Appraisal Form' which was used to assess the doctors' performance in the role plays (see Figure 6.4). Most sessions focused on a particular stage of the consultation and features of language use salient to that stage. So, for example, Week 8 focused on the stage, Offering and Explaining a Diagnosis, language for expressing medical terminology in alternative ways and the use of conditionals. The topics covered each week in the English classes were organized to coincide with the topics being covered in the professional development component of the course. Each English class also included a role play practice activity following the themes in the professional development sessions. For these role play activities the ESP teacher devised paired role play cards. Figure 6.5 shows the Content pages from the front of the *Handbook of Course Materials*.

The two-pronged strategy

Within this broad structure, the instruction was based on a 'two-pronged' strategy – feedback on or response to the students' performance (present situation needs) and input on expert language use (target situation needs) (see Figure 6.6).

Skill	Not achieved				Achieved to level of 5th year medical student				Achieved with excellence
	0	2	4	6	8	10
Establishes initial rapport Build the relationship						
Establishes patient's concern Understands patient's perspective						
Explores and clarifies from medical perspective						
Explores physical, social and psychological factors						
Provides structure to the consultation Pacing, flow, logical sequence, closure						
Offers and explains diagnosis, provides information						
Shares decision making; offers options To achieve a clear management plan						
Sensitive to patient's views; checks back and encourages patient to contribute						

Figure 6.4 Observed Consultation Appraisal Form

Skill	Not achieved			Achieved to level of 5th year medical student		Achieved with excellence
English proficiency (Actor's ease in understanding the candidate)	Unable to be understood	Very difficult to understand	Some difficulty in understanding	Able to be understood	Easily understood	Like talking to a Kiwi (Native New Zealander) doctor
Insight into Performance	Very poor insight	Poor insight	Some insight	Reasonable insight	Good insight	Extremely insightful – all areas covered.

Record of verbal self-critique   Score   /100
Comments on insight into performance
Actor's comments
What was well done?
What was done less well?
Recommendations for improvement

Figure 6.4 Continued

Unit	Content
Introduction	Consultation Appraisal Form Criteria
	Language and Communication Skills

1. Greeting
   Connecting with the patient
   Opening the consultation

2. Establishing the patient's concerns
   Exploring and clarifying from a medical point of view
   Language: adjectives for feeling /pronunciation review (1)

3. Exploring and clarifying form a medical perspective (continued)
   Understanding the patient's perspective
   Language: verb tenses, pronunciation review (2)

4. Exploring and clarifying from a medical perspective (continued)
   Asking questions

5. Exploring and clarifying from a medical perspective (continued)
   Asking questions
   Talking about pain

6. Exploring and clarifying from a medical perspective
   Conversation repair strategies
   Signposting changes in direction

7. Exploring and clarifying from a medical perspective
   Asking about symptoms/systems
   Questions in sensitive areas: smoking/sex/drugs/alcohol

8. Offering and explaining a diagnosis
   Medical terminology alternatives
   Language: conditionals
   Video extract: Vanessa's story

9. Negotiating management
   Words to use with care
   "Quite' and other modifiers

10. Revision: explaining a diagnosis
    Expressing certainty & uncertainty
    Some/any

11. Revision: certainty & uncertainty
    Negotiating management & offering options
    'just'

12. Modal verbs
    Revision: negotiating management
    Offering encouragement & reassurance

Figure 6.5   Content page from the overseas-trained doctors' English language classes

Instructional strategy
— Feedback on students' performance in role plays
— Expert language use in the local context

Figure 6.6   Instructional strategy for the overseas-trained doctors' classes

Feedback on students' performance in role plays

A number of activities and tasks developed in the English course had arisen as response to problems observed either by the professional developers or by the ESP teacher in the overseas doctors' performance in the role plays. For example, having noticed some problems with use of tenses, the error-correction activity shown in Figure 6.7 was developed. It draws on problematic questions and statements made in the role plays.

But not all instruction responding to the doctors' performance was of such a black-and-white nature as shown in the 'grammar'-focus activity below. Often, the feedback was focused on 'more appropriate' language choices, and in order to understand what these were, the ESP teacher consulted the professional development trainers on a regular basis. For example, in one role play the patient had used the colloquial term 'back passage' but the doctor followed on by using the medical term 'rectum'. Consulting one of the trainers, the ESP teacher discovered that it is preferable in patient-centred consultations for the doctor to use the same terms as the patient. As part of the feedback focused instructional strategy developed for this course, the overseas-trained doctors could give the ESP teacher the video recording of their performance in the role play with the actor if they wished. The teacher would watch the video and make a set of personalized feedback notes on the doctor's use of language and communication strategies. For example, while watching the video recording the ESP teacher transcribed any occurrences of weak language choices or strategies and then suggested alternatives. However, this often required the teacher to talk to one of the professional development trainers to ask them what a good alternative expression or strategy would be, often couched in terms of 'how would you deal with this and what would you say in this situation?' In this way, the ESP teacher used the subject experts (the professional development trainers) as a linguistic resource for her input during feedback on the students' production.

Input on expert language use

The input comprised a number of activities and tasks aimed to draw the students' attention to features observed in expert language use, as seen in the authentic samples of discourse the ESP teacher had collected or in the models of

What's wrong with these questions and statements?	Are you having any allergies? Did you get any urine infection in the past? I'd like to do some tests and then I'll be having a clearer picture. You are having this pain for three weeks? If the migraine is come back, let me know.

Figure 6.7   Sample error-correction activity

language use the professional development trainers provided in their teaching. The activity shown in Figure 6.8 focuses on the use of open questions by one of the doctors in TV documentary material. In this activity, students listen to the video to fill in the gaps.

Each unit on the course had a language structure component focusing on a feature of language use related to the topic of the unit. Each unit also had a vocabulary component focusing on words and phrases related to the topic. The section of words and phrases was based on sources of specialist discourse such as the television medical documentary or the ESP teacher's observations of language use in doctor's clinics. In regard to the latter, the course materials focused on formulaic uses of language. The aim was to draw the overseas doctors' attention to the use of such formulaic expressions. The expressions had been observed by the ESP teacher time and again in the speaking of New Zealand and Australian trained doctors. The prefabricated chunks were thus 'grounded' samples of language for instruction. It was anticipated that the overseas doctors would be able to get a good deal of 'mileage' from being aware of these formulaic uses of the language. Figure 6.9 shows an example of material focusing on such prefabricated chunks. In this case, the samples are concerned with 'offering options' in negotiating management (treatment). Generally, the focus was linked to watching a video of a medical consultation in class. The

Video extract

Patient's name is Vanessa.

Consultation with a renal specialist 4 days after an operation.

1. How does the specialist ask about Vanessa's leg and toe? Note that the questions are open, fairly unspecified and neutral.

What's _____?
How's _____?
Are there _____walking?
The problems you've had with your legs, _____?
_____ your toe, _____?
It's _____. I'm _____optimistic.
Let's have a look at your hands, _____? Well it was certainly the right operation for you.

What's been happening here?
How's that going?
Are there any problems walking?
The problems you've had with your legs, how are they going?
What about your toe, how's that going?
It's not looking too bad.
I'm fairly optimistic.
Let's have a look at your hands, how's that going? Well it was certainly the right operation for you.

Figure 6.8 Drawing students' attention to features of language use and communication skills

Negotiating management – offering options

There are a few things we can do to help with …
What I'd like to suggest is …
I'd recommend … but it's up to you of course.
It would be a good idea to …
There are some things you can do to prevent …
How does that sound to you?
Do you have any thoughts on that?

Figure 6.9   Observing formulaic expressions

teacher asked the students to notice how the doctors used language for a particular function, encouraged them to recall other expressions they had heard and then drew their attention to formulaic expressions she had derived from her observations of speaking by doctors trained and practising in New Zealand and Australian contexts.

6.5   Responding to difficulties and constraints

Paradoxically, one of the difficulties the ESP teacher faced in this case was, as she saw it, at the same time an advantage. The difficulty was that the ESP teacher was not medically trained. This meant that she was on a steep learning curve in regard to developing her understanding of doctor medical discourse in patient–doctor consultations. The fact that she was not medically trained, however, was an advantage in that she was prevented from offering medical information or setting herself up as a source of medical communication expertise. She thus focused entirely on language use. Given that the students in this case were highly trained and experienced in their field, any attempts by a language teacher with a limited medical knowledge or some experience in medical communication to 'teach' medical content alongside language could have been seen as a source of irritation to the class. The flip side of the same coin was that the teacher needed to continually refer to the professional development trainers for information on medical communication. She was very aware that she could 'make no knowledge claims' on communication in the medical events and needed to check out the inferences she drew from her observations and analysis of specialist discourse with the professional development trainers.

The teacher felt that not being medically trained was an advantage in another respect – she was better able to notice features of language use in the medical communication that those within medical circles had limited awareness of and were largely impervious to. The professional development trainers could suggest a beautifully emphatic way of forming an utterance for a given medical scenario but could offer very little in the way of explanation or metalinguistic analysis on the forms used. Metalinguistic analysis is related to the distinction between implicit and explicit language knowledge. Implicit knowledge is unanalysed knowledge which the user is unaware of or cannot articulate. Explicit language knowledge is analysed knowledge which the user is aware of or can articulate (Ellis, 2005; Roehr, 2007, p. 179). The trainers were able to identify that there were some problems in the speaking of some of the overseas-trained doctors and that they might be able to correct the 'errors' by offering better language choices. However, the trainers could not articulate the rule behind the error or explain the rationale for the better choice. They tended to suggest 'blanket' advice for the overseas doctors such as 'just parrot what people say', and they could only offer 'vague' (and potentially inaccurate) assessments of the sources of the overseas doctors' language problems such as 'it's your pronunciation that's the problem' or 'your language – it's just too clunky'. However, as an outsider and one with a background in language studies, the ESP teacher was as in a far better position to notice features of language use as being distinctive to medical circles and was better able to analyse the sources of any difficulties in the language use of the overseas-trained doctors.

A second difficulty in the development of the English course for medical doctors was that of finding authentic source materials. Face-to-face interviews between doctors and their patients are by nature private and few ready-made recordings are available either for investigation of specialist discourse or for teaching purposes. Given this difficulty, a key element in the development of this course was the contacts made by the professional development trainers to help the ESP course teacher gain access and obtain the appropriate patient and doctors' consents and permission to observe medical consultations in general practice clinics.

6.6   Summary

The case study reported in this chapter was a course that focused on the patient-centred medical consultation, one very specific communicative event in medical practice. The need for the ESP course in this case arose from observations made before the ESP teacher/course developer was approached. It had been observed that a number of overseas-trained doctors taking the medical registration examination in a previous year had experienced difficulties in this specific event. The needs in this case were highly context specific: they were focused on patient-centred communication in New Zealand. As a result, the ESP teacher could not draw on descriptions of medical discourse from general 'English for Medical Doctors' type course books or even from research literature from the US or the UK. It was important for the teacher 'not to teach language use that was wrong or unacceptable in the local context'.

All of this meant that the ESP teacher had to examine discourse in the local context herself and arrive at her own understanding of the nature of discourse in the patient-centred medical consultation. However, as described above, although she had the language knowledge to analyse language use in the consultations, her lack of medical training prompted her to continually check her understanding of communication in these events with the domain experts, the professional development trainers. Once she had ascertained expectations of language use in the local context, she then 'diagnosed' the nature of the difficulties experienced by some of the overseas-trained doctors. She devised a course of instruction based on a two-pronged strategy of providing feedback on the 'diagnosed' areas of difficulty and 'treatment' in terms of information about language use (the input) that had been derived from her observations of authentic doctor–patient consultations in local settings.

6.7   Discussion

1. How would you classify the English for Patient-Centred Consultations Course in relation to the categorizations shown in Figure 1.1 (Areas of ESP Teaching) and Figure 1.2 (Time of Course in Relation to Experience)?
2. Where would you situate the course on the wide- and narrow-angled continuum discussed in Chapter 4?
3. The course described in this chapter was devised for a group of learners who were very close in time to 'end use' – that is to say, they were likely to be using the information they received from the English course in the very near future. In a situation like this, we might expect students to be receptive to very detailed information about language use and communication in the target situation (in comparison to students who are some time away from actual use). How important is it for ESP course developers to consider the proximity or distance of time to end use when determining the level of detail on target situation language use to provide in the course?
4. In preparing a general language teaching course, a good deal of work needs to be done 'up front' to determine the curriculum and prepare materials. This up front or 'lead-in time' is even more critical in ESP given that the teacher may need to investigate specialist discourse in addition to devising the curriculum and materials. In the case study reported in this chapter, the teacher had very limited lead-in time to prepare the course, and she had to investigate discourse at the same time as teaching the course for the first time. Think of an ESP course you may be required to develop in the future. How much lead-in time would you ideally like for preparation, how would you use it and how much time might you realistically be given?
5. Subject specialists may not have a sophisticated knowledge about language with which to describe meaningfully target situation language use and the nature of linguistic difficulties (Basturkmen, forthcoming). In the present case, the ESP teacher worked closely with subject specialists – the professional

development trainers. However, as described above, although these subject specialists were able to identify that there were problems in the language use of some of the overseas doctors, they were not able to be precise about the nature of these difficulties. Similarly, although they were able to provide samples of appropriate language use, they were not able to analyse or offer explicit description of the features of appropriate language use. In other words, their knowledge of language use in the consultations was largely tacit. How exactly did this impact on how the ESP teacher worked with the professional development trainers? What ways can you think of to derive information on learners' needs or target situation language use from subject specialists who do not have sophisticated knowledge about language?

6. In what ways and to what extent can the approach to investigation of specialist discourse in this case be described as ethnographic? Review the discussion of this term in Chapter 3.

7. The use of a published course book was not an option for the ESP teacher in this case given that the overseas doctors needed to become familiar with how the medical consultations were practised in the local context. Is there a relationship between the level of specificity of an ESP course and the adoption of a published course book as opposed to the development of in-house materials?

8. Many of the activities involved in the 'English for Doctors' course required the students to make close observations and analysis of samples of language use. Do such activities appear related to the learning style of medical doctors? How important is the selection of types of learning activity in the development of ESP courses?

Acknowledgements

I would like to thank Rosemary Wette of the Department of Applied Language and Linguistics at the University of Auckland for allowing me to report the development of the course reported in this chapter. I am very grateful to her for generously allowing me access to the materials and information in this case study. I would also express my gratitude to Sue Lawton and Richard Fox of the School of Medicine, the University of Auckland.

7
Academic Literacies in Visual Communication

The present chapter examines the development of a course in the area of English for Visual Arts Studies, a course that is a component of a foundation art and design studies programme in a university context. In a number of ways this case stands apart from those described in the previous two chapters. The cases examined in Chapters 5 and 6 focused on *workplace* language needs and English for professional purposes. This chapter focuses on language needs for *study purposes*. The course described in Chapter 5 was a *during-experience* course. It was taken by the police recruits at the same time that they were working and gaining experience of policing. The course examined in Chapter 6 was a *post-experience* course. It was designed for students who were all practised medical doctors. The doctors already had medical (disciplinary) knowledge and were familiar with the kinds of communicative events employed in the target situation. The case reported in the present chapter is a *pre-experience* course and the students in this course were new to art and design studies. Thus they had limited disciplinary knowledge and were relatively unfamiliar with the genres, especially the written genres that were important for their studies. The 'pre-experience' ESP course described in this chapter set out to provide disciplinary content as well as language content.

Unlike the developers of the courses described in the previous two chapters, the teacher/course developer in the present case was himself a subject specialist. His first degree had been in Fine Arts, and, at the same time that he was teaching the Academic Literacies in Visual Communication (ALVC) course, he was also teaching 'studio' (a course in which students design a visual work of art). As will be evident in this chapter, these points of difference influenced what the teacher/course developer included in the course and the approach he used.

Furthermore, discourse in this field, that is, Visual Arts, is in some ways distinct from discourse in other fields and is certainly quite different from the discourse in the previous two case studies. Visual Arts is a subject much associated with abstraction and creativity. In the two previous case studies (English for Police and English for Medical Doctors) the investigation of discourse and ESP instruction focused largely on conventionalized patterns of language use. Both of these fields are associated with material evidence. But is language use in a creative and abstract field such as Visual Arts similarly conventionalized? How can discourse in such an abstract and creative subject be translated into ESP course content?

The organization of the chapter follows that of the previous two chapters. Section 7.1 describes the context of the course. Sections 7.2 and 7.3 describe the investigation of needs and specialist discourse respectively. Section 7.4 describes and illustrates the course and the materials. Finally, section 7.5 identifies the difficulties and constraints encountered in the development of the course.

7.1 Context

The ALVC course had been preceded by a general skills-based writing course. This section describes the situation which led to the development of the ALVC course. Like the ALVC course, the original general skills-based course was developed for students on a university certificate programme in visual arts. The certificate programme ran over one academic year and in this context served as a foundation year and route to entry into the bachelor degree programme. At that time a core component of the certificate programme was an art theory course, a course focusing on theoretical concepts in the History of Art. International students from a range of countries and geographical areas including China and South East Asia and for whom English is a second language, comprised a sizeable proportion of students on the certificate and bachelor's programmes.

The original general skills-based writing course had focused on developing generic academic writing skills and used topics from visual arts. It had been developed by the EAP section of the university but for various reasons was taken over by the Art and Design Faculty. Later on the head of the Art and Design Certificate Program approached the teacher/course developer in the present case and asked him to develop a new English course (15 credit points) to support the international students on the certificate programme. The 'international students' would attend the English course while the 'home' students attended life-drawing classes.

The teacher/course developer had taught English for Arts and Design in a UK university and had become disenchanted with the general skills-based approach in EAP because he found it of limited value in helping students with writing in their discipline. Thus when the teacher was asked to develop a course for the visual arts students, he decided to focus the course on writing in visual arts, that is, disciplinary writing and not general writing skills. He devised a course drawing on genre theory and perspectives from the literature on academic literacies (for example, Lea, 2004) and began teaching it.

However, students on the certificate programme continued to struggle with the art theory course. They found it difficult to understand the content of the course and the requirements of the assignments they needed to write. In conjunction with colleagues, the teacher therefore redeveloped the ALVC course. The new course became a 30-credit point course that would cater for both international and home-based students. The most radical change was that the new version of the course would combine English teaching with disciplinary content from art theory/art history. Since the teacher had studied Fine Arts he would draw on his disciplinary knowledge to include subject content into the course. The focus of the course was to prepare the students for the language-based academic practices involved in their programme of study.

7.2 Investigating needs

As discussed in Chapter 3, needs analysis does not necessarily start from scratch, analysts may draw on findings of previous needs analyses in similar settings. In this case, the teacher/course developer's understanding of needs was based on his experiences and observations over years of teaching English for Arts and Design studies. For example, in developing the ALVC course the teacher/course developer drew on an investigation he had begun when teaching English to Art and Design students at a university in UK. In this investigation he had analysed samples of students' writing. He had compared essays which had been given high grades with those given low grades by the Arts faculty and he looked at the subject lecturers' feedback comments on them. He had tried to identify what the subject lecturers valued and the nature of student difficulties in writing. In addition, drawing on genre theory he had analysed the essays for their typical content, organization in terms of moves and linguistic features.

In the local context (the certificate programme in visual arts), students had difficulties in understanding the content of the art theory course and struggled with the course assignments. They found the reading texts and the lectures simply too difficult. The art theory course required a good deal of background knowledge. For example, one of the topics on the art theory course the students found difficult was 'Modernism in the New Zealand Context'. The lectures and texts tended to assume that the students were familiar with the concepts of modernism and could understand it in a European historical context. But very often this was not the case. The gaps in the students' knowledge and understanding caused students to 'struggle with both the content and the writing component of the Art Theory course'. Moreover, the students' difficulties in the core art theory course had implications in turn for their performance in other courses on the certificate programme, including the 'theoretically driven' studio course in which students work on design projects. These difficulties were reported by students and subject lecturers alike and led to the teacher's decision to expand the ALVC course so that it would introduce subject content alongside language (literacy) content. This decision, taken in consultation with colleagues in the Art and Design faculty, resulted in a course in which discipline-specific writing was taught side by side with art theory/art history (subject content).

To sum up, the decision to refocus the course was based on a combination of factors: the teacher's experiences of teaching English to students of Arts and Design, the difficulties the students experienced in their art theory course and the teacher's theoretical orientation which, informed by genre theory and the literature on academic literacies, implied that academic writing cannot be separated from disciplinary content.

7.3   Investigating specialist discourse

Writing is the major, although not exclusive, focus of the ALVC course. This section describes how the teacher investigated discourse and presents some of the features of written discourse the ALVC course focuses on. To identify these features the teacher/course developer drew in part on the investigation of student essays he had started while working in the UK. This investigation provided indications of how to proceed with the ALVC paper development. (Some results from this study can be seen in Turner and Hocking, 2004.) At that time, research into discourse of visual arts as a discipline had been very limited. The teacher therefore conducted his own investigations and drew on his previous work examining academic discourse and communication in visual arts (Hocking, 2004). The teacher investigated discourse through what he referred to as 'both subject and language perspectives'. In other words, he examined texts in visual arts focusing on what was written about, the aims of writing, how language was used and the types of perspectives valued within this academic discipline.

One focus of this investigation was on how writers in visual arts discuss the interaction between theory and practice. A good deal of importance is given to this discussion in the discipline and it is an important element in how students' writing is evaluated. It is expected that writers will articulate how practice (such as an existing painting or sculpture, or a student's work of art) relates to theory (such as post-structuralist or feminist theory). In the case of an existing work of art, theory is often used to *explain* features of the work (the practice) and in the case of the student's own art work, theory is often called on to *justify* features. Excerpt 1 shows part of an interview in which the teacher/course developer describes how theory is used in writing about practice in visual arts.

Excerpt 1

TEACHER: Students use theory, say post-structuralist theory, to unpack what they are doing in their art work – if it's their own art work, to justify what they are doing and if it's someone else's, to come to a conclusion about what is happening in the work.

INTERVIEWER: Are they using the theory as a framework for analysis of practice? Are they explaining the practice as being the way it is because of the theoretical ideas?

TEACHER: It's much looser than that. The theory could be anything, say something around feminist identity. If you're looking at the structure of the art work there's a kind of intertwining between theory and practice. The theory serves to illustrate something that's going on in the practice. ... The students' writing is performative. They are performing as they write and staking out identities.

The use of theory to 'unpack' (or analyse) a work of art is illustrated in a text developed for the ALVC course (see Figure 7.1). The text shows the beginning of an analysis of a painting by the artist, Malevich. The text analyses the painting in relation to Modernist theory (moving away from representation and towards abstraction).

Writing as performance is related to the idea that a person's identity is socially constructed. In this view, identity is formed through how the person uses language and other forms of expression to represent his or her identity and beliefs. Paltridge (2006) gives the example of rap singers whose choice of what to rap about, use of language and self-presentation all contribute to their performance and creation of themselves as rap singers. However, the creative use of writing as performance does not mean to say that writing is an entirely free form of expression. Gee (2005) describes discourse as a dance:

> A Discourse is a 'dance' that exists in the abstract as a coordinated pattern of words, deeds, values, beliefs, symbols, tools, objects, times, and places in the here and now as a performance that is recognizable as just such a coordination. Like a dance, the performance here and now is never exactly the same. It all comes down, often, to what the 'masters of the dance' will allow to be recognised as a possible instantiation of the dance. (Gee, 2005, 19)

Malevich's work titled 'Suprematist Composition: Red Square and Black Square' from 1915 exemplifies many aspects of modernist thought. The work consists of a black square and a smaller red square on a white canvass. The black square sits above the red square, which is slightly off-axis and sits on its left-hand corner. The work can be seen from a purely modernist attempt to move away from academic representation towards the purely abstract by examining the relationship between pure geometric form, colour and space. Like other modernists Malevich linked his move away from academic representation with the utopian vision of the communist revolution.

Figure 7.1   Text from the ALVC course handbook

The quotation juxtaposes the creative use of language (language as performance of a dance) and the constraining role of social expectations (the dance is only a dance if the masters of the dance recognize the performance as such). The ALVC teacher described this juxtaposition in terms of the 'tension' facing visual arts student writers. On the one hand they are expected to write creatively and critically (to *perform* as they write and *stake out their identities*), but on the other hand their creative ideas need to be written in ways that meet disciplinary expectations (ways that will be recognized as *acceptable instantiations*). One of the aims of the ALVC course is to introduce students to the academic genres of writing to raise their awareness of 'acceptable instantiations' in the eyes of the members of the visual arts discipline in that context.

Further features of discourse in visual arts and contrasts with discourse in sciences include:

- Poetic, imaginative and playful modes of writing.
- Multi-model nature of discourse, often with visual images used alongside written text.
- Writing may highlight an emotional response and reflect that the writer's emotions as well as mind are engaged.
- Particular citations may be foregrounded.
- Writing is not judged according to criteria of accessibility and clarity, the 'transparent traditional forms of academia' so highly valued in scientific writing.
- The principles of rationality and objectiveness embraced in scientific discourse do not apply. (Turner and Hocking, 2004, p. 157)

Examples 1 and 2 illustrate some of these features. The use of *enthusiasm, investment* and *interest* signal the emotional response of the writer. The writer refers to a particularly lengthy quote. The writer is not trying to be 'objective'. The writer rejects an art-critical stance of 'disinterest' (which might be expected by a writer oriented to art theory 'modernist' perspectives) (Turner and Hocking, 2004, pp. 155–6).

Example 1

'Please allow in my *enthusiasm* the following long quote …'.

Example 2

'In this essay, I set out to establish my *investment* or current *interest* in …'.

Writing in this discipline is particularly dense and complex. According to the teacher/course developer 'what is interesting here (and we look at this with students) is the poetic density of early 20th century art historical prose ... it's often impenetrable and ironically this is the sort of text that students go to first because of familiarity and because they think it will be easy'.

According to the course developer writing in this discipline has received less research interest than writing in natural and social science disciplines. When the ALVC course was first devised, published description of discourse in the field was very limited. Very little empirical research into visual arts genres from the perspective of EAP was available. More recently, the journal, *Writing for Creative Practice*, has been launched and further descriptions have thus become available.

7.4   Designing the course and materials

Ending the separation of disciplinary content and writing

The ALVC course runs over two semesters (one full academic year). It combines disciplinary subject content (art theory/history) with a focus on language features of written discourse in the visual arts and on the genres that visual arts students read and write. Examples of the genres students write are 'Descriptions and Analyses of Art Works' and the 'Exegesis'. (The Exegesis is the written or spoken text the student devises to support or justify his or her own design or visual production.) The course is based on the view that writing and disciplinary subject content should not be separated. According to the teacher/ course developer, 'You cannot take the subject out of writing.' These ideas can be related to the literature on ESAP. Hyland describes the discipline-specific concept of discourse saying:

> Disciplines and professions are largely created and maintained through distinctive ways that members construct a view of the world through their discourses. What counts as convincing argument, appropriate tone, persuasive interaction, and so on, is managed for a particular audience. (Hyland, 2009, p. 203)

The ALVC course is thematically organized into four periods of art history: Renaissance, Enlightenment, Modernism and Post-Modernism. Part of the course outline (adapted) is shown in Figure 7.2.

A set of principles allied to the theoretical literature on genre theory and academic literacies, in particular the writing of Lea (2004) and Lea and Street (1998), influenced the design of the curriculum. The course aims to take into account students' present and previous literacy practices and to raise students'

Renaissance and Enlightenment	
Week	Topic
1	Introduction to ALVC
2	Genres of Writing
3	The Essay Writing Process
4	The Renaissance: Overview and Writing Summaries
5	Renaissance: Humanism & Writing Definitions
6	Mercantilism & Tasman's Discovery of * Zeelandia Nova
7	Mercantilism/Writing Description and Analysis
8	The Increasing Social Status of the Artist
9	Science and Reason (Enlightenment thought)
10	Landscape and the Sublime
Non teaching studio week	
Modernism	
11	Industrialization
12	Disenchantment and Crisis
13	The Paradigm of Modernism
14	Revolution and Abstraction/Structures of Critical Writing
15	The Essay Question/Writing Introductions and Conclusions
16	Modern Design and Functionalism
17	Functionalism – A Critique/Structures of Critical Writing
18	Psychoanalysis & the Subconscious
Non teaching studio week	
Post-Modernism	
19	Choosing the Right Citation
20	From Modernism to Postmodernism
21	Hyper-Reality and Representation
22	The Exegesis

Figure 7.2 Part of the ALVC course outline
Note: *A term used in earlier times to denote 'New Zealand'.

awareness of difficulties they might face in negotiating the textual demands of their academic studies. The principles included:

1. considering students' prior textual experiences and subject knowledge,
2. focusing on socio-historic practices and beliefs informing contemporary understanding of the subject,
3. exploring genres and textual practices to foster students' understanding of socio-historic practices and beliefs,
4. making disciplinary and institutional expectations for writing transparent
5. creating dialogue around identity and cultural differences. (Hocking and Fieldhouse, 2005)

The remainder of this section of the chapter illustrates the ways in which some of these principles were incorporated into the design of the course and the materials.

Principle: Considering students' prior textual experiences and subject knowledge

In designing the course the teacher bore in mind the kinds of texts in visual arts that students were likely to have read before beginning their university studies. He tried to find out what they had read and what kinds of understanding of the field they were likely to have derived from this reading. In particular, he tried to identify any understandings that were likely to be 'disjunctures',[1] that is, 'at odds with' contemporary perspectives within the academic discipline. For example, given that the students entering the ALVC course were new to visual arts as an academic subject, they were likely to have read mainly traditional art historical or biographical books, the kind of books many laypeople have on the bookshelf at home. The writing in such works varies from the writing expected in academic visual arts settings. For example, traditional art historical or biographical works often portray the artist as the 'creative individual' or a 'genius' rather than as an active producer of artistic forms. This conception of the 'creative individual' has of late been widely critiqued in academic circles, although the critique has not been disseminated into the wider culture (Hocking and Fieldhouse, 2005).

Because of the potential for student understandings to be at odds with contemporary perspectives within the academic discipline, the ALVC course exposes students to a range of visual arts genres (such as theoretical works, essays and other professional genres as well as art history and biographical texts) so that the students can see alternative conceptions of disciplinary knowledge. In addition, the course involves discussion in class about these genres and how they have been influenced by the ideologies and the socio-historical contexts of their writers. Returning to the example of the conception of the artist as a creative genius, the course includes a text from the art theory literature which details how the fascination of Renaissance artists for the mathematics of perspective stemmed from a desire to elevate their image, work and personal status from the idea of 'craftsmanship'. The text is used alongside a second text taken from a popular art-historical book. The latter describes the development of perspective as the inspiration of Renaissance 'genius'. This principle of using different texts to provide students with a range of beliefs and socio-historic contexts that have influenced art production is an important feature in the course design.

Principle: Exploring genres and textual practices and making disciplinary expectations for writing transparent

Figure 7.3 shows some of the genre-focused writing materials developed for the course. The material is taken from a unit that looks at structures of critical writing. The unit discusses a painting titled 'Black Square and Red Square' by Kasimir Malevich (1915). This painting is from an early movement of Modernism referred to as Constructivism. The unit begins with a reading about the painting from the art theory literature (not shown in the figure). Students are required to

In your essay you will analyse the work of a modernist practitioner and state why the work exemplifies modernist aesthetics or ideologies. One problem of this type of 'practice → theory' writing is that you could fall into the trap of being **too descriptive**. It is important that you concentrate on developing your own theoretical and critical perspectives which are often based on the ideas of others (through disagreement, agreement or questioning). Of course, writing about visual works will also involve a degree of description as well, but this is used to develop a more critical perspective. Look at the example below:

Example

Malevich's work titled 'Suprematist Composition: Red Square and Black Square' from 1915 exemplifies many aspects of modernist thought. The work consists of a black square and a smaller red square on a white canvass. The black square sits above the red square, which is slightly off-axis and sits on its left-hand corner. The work can be seen from a purely modernist attempt to move away from academic representation towards the purely abstract by examining the relationship between pure geometric form, colour and space. Like other modernists Malevich linked his move away from academic representation with the utopian vision of the communist revolution; a 'new revolutionary art appropriate for the new revolutionary society.' (Harrison & Wood, 1992; p. 221) In Malevich's 1920 essay 'The question of Imitative Art' he states that:

Many people think that anything except communism is beneficial to the people; the same sort of people think that only academicism can produce real art; both are cases of blindness to their own real perfection (Malevich, p. 294).

As a result, I believe the black square of 'Suprematist Composition' might represent the oppressive nature of pre-Revolutionary Russia while the off-axis red square could be interpreted as the youthful communist revolution not adhering to traditional ideology.
References

Malevich, K. (1992) The Question of Imitative Art, in C Harrison and P Wood (eds), *Art in Theory: 1900–1990.* Oxford: Blackwell (pp. 292–7).
Harrison, C. & Wood, P. (1992). *Art in Theory: 1900–1990.* Oxford: Blackwell.

Instructions

1. Identify the sentence that sets up or initiates this discussion.
2. Identify the purely descriptive parts of the text.
3. Identify the theoretical/analytical parts of the text. What do these consist of?
4. Identify the 'result claim' that combines the descriptive and analytical to come to an interesting conclusion

Malevich's work titled 'Suprematist Composition: Red Square and Black Square' from 1915 exemplifies many aspects of modernist thought.	**Highlighting statement** Sets up or initiates this section of the essay or current discussion.
The work consists of a black square and a smaller red square on a white canvass. The black square sits above the red square, which is slightly off-axis and sits on its left-hand corner.	**Description** Describes the work/section of the work under discussion. This could also involve quotes.

Figure 7.3   Course material on structures of critical writing
Source: Material from Academic Literacies in Visual Communication Course

The work can be seen from a purely modernist attempt to move away from academic representation towards the purely abstract by examining the relationship between pure geometric form, colour and space. Like other modernists Malevich linked his move away from academic representation with the utopian vision of the communist revolution; a 'new revolutionary art appropriate for the new revolutionary society.' (Harrison & Wood, 1992; p. 221) In Malevich's 1920 essay 'The question of Imitative Art' he states that: Many people think that anything except communism is beneficial to the people; the same sort of people think that only academicism can produce real art; both are cases of blindness to their own real perfection (Malevich, p. 294).	**Background** **Theory/Analysis** Uses a mixture of the writer's own knowledge, quotes, paraphrases and summaries to provide a theoretical perspective.
As a result, I believe the black square of 'Suprematist Composition' might represent the oppressive nature of pre-Revolutionary Russia while the off-axis red square could be interpreted as the youthful communist revolution not adhering to traditional ideology.	**Result claim** Concludes with a result or critical development of the discussion.

Consider the works below in relation to Malevich's painting:

1. Boris Eremeevich Vladimiriski 'Roses for Stalin' (1949).
2. Record cover for the Scottish band Franz Ferdinand (2005).

Writing Task

Using the artwork you selected earlier as a subject, write a similar text to the one just analysed. Use the grid below as a guide.

...........................'s work .... exemplifies aspects of the aesthetic concerns of modernism.	Highlighting statement
The work consists of.	Description
The work can be seen as	Background Theory/Analysis
In this sense	Result claim What do *you* think? Try and relate the theory to the description if possible.
References	

Figure 7.3   Continued

read the text and make notes on Malevich's aesthetic and ideological outlooks. Figure 7.3 shows the next section from the material. This section focuses on how critical writing can be structured. It presents an 'analysis' of the painting. (The 'analysis' is a written genre in visual arts studies.) The material shows the sequence of moves in the analysis and describes the function of the moves. The material also illustrates how a writer can incorporate his or her own theoretical and critical perspective into the analysis.

7.5 Responding to difficulties and constraints

Developing the ALVC course was time consuming. A major cause of this was the need to develop descriptions of discourse for the course. Descriptions of discourse in visual arts are relatively few and far between. Art theory featured far less in visual arts in the past (for example, when the teacher/course developer in this case did his first degree in Fine Arts the degree did not involve an art theory course), and expectations for students' writing in theory-based arts subjects are still emerging. The teacher/course developer thus had little by way of 'ready to go' description of writing to draw on when devising the ALVC course. In order to find out about discourse in theoretical subjects in visual arts studies, the teacher/course developer (sometimes in conjunction with colleagues) conducted investigations into discourse. But investigating discourse is time consuming. At the time of devising the ALVC course, the teacher/course developer was working on a doctorate in the field of discourse analysis. He was thus able to draw on descriptions from his own academic studies in developing the course.

As we have seen, the course involves genre-based descriptions (such as that illustrated in Figure 7.3). However, the teacher was concerned that students might get the impression that such descriptions are prescriptions that they should adopt uncritically. This concern created tension. On the one hand the teacher wanted the course to make the institutional and disciplinary expectations for writing clear but on the other hand he wished to avoid the possibility that the students might think that the 'structures of the genres students write for assessment should be uncritically modelled or conceptualised as unalterable forms' (Hocking and Fieldhouse, 2005, pp. 3–4). This tension can be related to arguments in the EAP literature. Should EAP simply aim to help students become *socialized* into the discourse practices of their academic discipline or should it also help students contest those discourse practices and voice their own identities? Hyland (2006) in defining these two perspectives writes:

> *Socialization.* Orienting learners to the genres, norms and practice of particular disciplines, familiarizing them with the ways it constructs knowledge and what it values in writing and communication. The notion of 'access' is central, although it is often seen as something students need to adjust to. *Literacies.* Assisting learners to engage in, understand and critique the discursive practices and epistemologies of their fields, recognizing the complexity and specificity of those fields and their effects on individual identities. (Hyland, 2006, p. 223)

The academic socialization model of EAP assumes that students need to learn the norms and conventions in their new academic discipline or culture. An academic literacies approach suggests that attempting to mimic disciplinary approved forms of discourse can create serious problems for many students. Because they have to use language in unfamiliar ways their choices of expression are restricted and their own opinions, experiences and identities are devalued. This can mean that students present a persona that feels alien to them. (Hyland, 2006, p. 226)

To resolve this and other issues the teacher drew *selectively* on principles from literature on academic literacies. The students in the certificate programme, he felt, were not yet in a position to contest the 'approved forms of discourse' (they were unfamiliar with the discourse and content of visual arts studies). The course he devised therefore aimed to make institutional and disciplinary expectations clear to the students, expose them to a range of visual arts genres and help them acquire disciplinary subject knowledge. This would provide them with a knowledge base from which they would be able to 'contest the dominant discourse practices' and voice their own identities in the future.

7.6   Summary

The present chapter focused on the development of an ESAP course (English for Visual Arts Studies). As stated in the introduction to this chapter, this case is quite different from the preceding cases: it is a pre-experience course and in developing it the teacher took into account the limited knowledge the students had of the discipline. A further point of difference lies in the teacher's background. This teacher was a subject specialist himself. Not only had he studied visual arts to degree level he was also teaching an arts 'studio' course at the time he developed and taught the ALVC course. These factors as well as the teacher's theoretical perspectives which were informed by genre theory and the literature on academic literacies explain why a course integrating disciplinary and language content was developed.

The introduction asked whether discourse in this particular discipline could be described in terms of conventional textual patterns and prevalent language features. It would seem that it can 'to an extent'. The features of discourse in this discipline certainly appear to be more elusive than those in science, yet investigations have revealed some characteristic textual patterns and features of language use. And, as was shown in this chapter, these characteristic features have been translated into instructional materials.

7.7   Discussion

1. The general skills-based approach to teaching writing in EAP is based on the idea that there is a generic set of skills and rhetorical patterns that is used across different disciplines. However, writers such as Hyland (2006) question the

usefulness of this approach and argue that the writing students need to learn is discipline-specific. Similarly, the teacher in this case argues that writing and subject content cannot be separated. What are your views on this topic?

2. The teacher in this case was a subject specialist in that he had studied visual arts. He was thus able to combine disciplinary subject content with language content in designing and teaching the course. Another possibility for integrating subject and language content is team teaching. In team teaching the EAP teacher (the language specialist) works alongside a content teacher/lecturer (a subject specialist). For example, in teaching English for legal studies, the students may be given a reading text and comprehension questions on it (a text for example from a law textbook). In class the lecturers/teachers and students review the students' answers to the questions. The EAP teacher deals with queries and corrections of language items and highlights language features in the text and the law lecturer deals with queries and corrections of the students' answers in terms of their understanding of legal content and highlights points of law. How important is it, do you think, to integrate disciplinary and language content? In which situations is it feasible?

3. One method of investigating disciplinary expectations for students' writing is to examine students' essays and lecturer feedback comments on them. It is also possible to supplement this with interviews with subject lecturers to discuss their expectations and values concerning writing in their discipline. It would also be possible to discuss samples of students' writing in the interview and ask the lecturers to explain why they responded to the writing as they did. Plan a *hypothetical* project investigating disciplinary expectations for students' writing:

Which discipline would you investigate?

Who would the students be (first year, final year, postgraduate)?

How many courses and written assignment tasks would you focus on (all, some, one)?

How many samples of writing would you examine?

How would you analyse the samples of student writing?

Would you use interviews? If so, who would you interview and what would you ask?

Note

1. In the literature on academic literacies, Lea (2004, p. 746) refers to 'disjunctures' between students' understandings and institutional or disciplinary expectations.

Acknowledgement

I would like to thank Darryl Hocking of AUT University, Auckland for generously giving his time and for providing access and information on the development of the course described in this chapter.

8
English for Thesis Writing

The final case study concerns a set of workshops developed to meet the needs of students who are writing up theses and dissertations. (In the remainder of this chapter, the term, thesis, will be used to refer to theses and dissertations.) The majority of students attending the workshops are writing a thesis for the first time and do not have experience of writing this particular academic 'genre'. The case is similar to the case reported in Chapter 6 in that the workshops have been developed to prepare students for one specific communicative situation. The course described in Chapter 6 focused a speaking situation (the patient-centred medical consultation). The workshop series you will read about in the present chapter focuses on a specific type of writing, the thesis report.

The thesis is of critical importance to students who conduct a research study for their degree. The thesis is the 'public record' of the research the student conducted for a master or doctoral degree and it will be examined both internally (within the university) and externally (by one or more examiners at a second university). The thesis represents the culmination of an extended period of study. By the time the student comes to writing up the thesis, he or she will have already invested a good deal of time, effort and care in designing and carrying out the research. The thesis needs to reflect the student's investment of time and effort as well as his or her understanding of the literature on the topic of research and on research methodology in general. In the case of students doing their masters, the thesis usually carries more 'credits' than any course-work paper. (In some cases, the master degree is done entirely by thesis.) In the case of students doing doctorates, the thesis is often the pathway to an academic career. All in all, the students are keen to get their theses 'up to scratch' in terms of meeting academic expectations and ensuring the reports reflect the quality of their research.

The reader will by now be familiar with the five-part organization of the case study chapters. Section 8.1 describes the context. Sections 8.2 and 8.3 describe the teacher/course developer's investigation of needs and specialist discourse respectively. Section 8.4 examines the design and presents illustrative materials. Section 8.5 examines the difficulties the case presented and how the teacher/ course developer responded to these difficulties. As with the previous chapters, this chapter ends with questions for discussion.

8.1   Context

The workshop series is situated in a university context. It has been developed to cater for students from a range of disciplines including language and communication, health, business studies, humanities and art and creative technologies. A considerable proportion of the students in this context are non-native speakers of English (the university attracts students from within the country and internationally).

The series originated in a one-off workshop on 'writing the thesis literature review' that the teacher (who lectures and conducts research in Applied Linguistics) offered for postgraduate students at his university. The workshop was held on the weekend so that students from any discipline and especially those who were working at the same time as they were studying would be able to attend. In this context, a considerable proportion of research students were 'mature' students who studied part time.

The idea for the original workshop arose from a combination of two factors. Firstly, the postgraduate centre at the university had become aware that a common problem for thesis writing students was how to formulate their 'literature chapter'. The literature chapter, or the 'Literature Review', is often the longest chapter in a thesis and requires a good deal of consideration about its organization and content. From informal channels, the postgraduate centre had heard from students and their supervisors that this chapter was an area of difficulty. Secondly, the teacher in this case was conducting his own research into parts and chapters of the thesis from a genre perspective (each part or chapter was seen as a genre in its own right). Additionally, the teacher was trying to help his own research students in writing their literature reviews as they found this a particularly difficult chapter. This research interest of the teacher came to the attention of the postgraduate centre, and since the topic coincided with an area of 'need' for a number of students in different disciplines, the graduate centre asked the teacher if he would offer a one-off workshop on 'writing the literature review' to students from any department across the university who would like to attend.

Since the workshop was to be held during the weekend and was an open-access arrangement, there were some 'unknowns'. It was not known at first whether students would be willing to devote part of their weekend to this subject; which students would be likely to turn up – master or doctoral students; and whether the workshop would attract students from some specific disciplines rather than others (for example, from humanities rather than business studies). It was also not known whether students would find the workshop useful. Given that the content of the workshop was not discipline-specific, that is, it did not target writing in the particular disciplines in which the students were conducting research, would the students find the information relevant?

This scenario presented quite a challenge for the teacher in terms of designing the workshop. Having investigated the literature review in his own research from a genre perspective, the teacher decided that some form of genre-based description, using examples from theses in Applied Linguistics but discussing them with reference to the other disciplines represented by students who were likely to attend the workshop, would be a sensible design option. The genre-based description would be the 'common denominator' and he would lead discussion around similarities and differences in the various disciplines.

Needless to say, the workshop proved highly successful and it attracted both masters and doctoral students and students from a range of disciplines. The evaluation forms completed by students after the workshop along with informal feedback, which included comments by students and supervisors, indicated that students and supervisors perceived a need for more such workshops. It seemed the 'literature review' was only one of the chapters that students needed help with. These were the seeds of the 'workshop series' on thesis writing that is the subject of the remainder of this chapter.

8.2   Investigating needs

This case presented a somewhat unusual situation for the needs analysis since the workshop series to be offered, like the first workshop session described above, was to be 'open access'. It was also not to be a 'course' of study. Rather the students could elect to attend if they wished, they could elect to attend some sessions rather than others, they could attend just part of a session, and it was expected that students would attend on a 'as needs' basis (their needs at the time). That is, if the student was writing the methodology chapter, he or she might elect to attend the sessions on 'writing the methods chapter' and possibly the session on 'reporting results'. Or another doctoral student, starting out on his or her research might elect to attend the session on 'writing a proposal' and possibly, writing the introduction (the chapter that sets out the aims and rationale for the study) but might not wish to attend sessions on writing the results and the discussion of results sessions until the following year. Since the students were all at different stages in their research, their needs and interests varied.

Another complicating factor was that not all students (and supervisors) perceived that students needed help equally with all sections of the thesis. Some chapters, such as the 'Discussion of Results', were widely seen as problematic whereas others, such as the 'Introduction', were not. Moreover there was a range of types of difficulties. Some students who were not native speakers of English had difficulties at a linguistic level (in terms of sentence structure and vocabulary choice). Some native and non-native speaker students had difficulties in expressing complex ideas and information clearly. And, as supervisors reported, students varied greatly in terms of their awareness of academic expectations for the form and content of the various sections of the thesis. A further complicating factor was that the students were undertaking a range of research studies, different not only in terms of disciplinary areas but also in terms of whether the studies were quantitative or qualitative, descriptive or experimental, and this impacted to an extent on their needs. The thesis of a qualitative study may be organized somewhat differently from that of a quantitative study (Mackey and Gass, 2005).

In short, the 'target' audience for the sessions in this case was not fixed since the class members were likely to change over the duration of the workshop series. Thus there was not one clearly delineated group of learners whose 'needs' would be identified as the basis of the design of the workshop series.

Chapter 2 discussed options for investigating needs that are available to course developers. One option was to consult the literature to find out what previous research has shown about needs in similar situations. Chapter 2 argued that this option can be overlooked as course developers may endeavour to 'start from scratch' in investigating needs. In the present case, this option was an important source of information for the teacher. The teacher consulted the considerable body of literature on the topic (for example, Cooley and Lewkowicz, 2003; Rudestam and Newton, 2001; Evans and Gruba, 2002; Hart, 2005; Paltridge and Starfield, 2007). He also consulted studies investigating students' difficulties in writing at the postgraduate level. For example, research by Cooley and Lewkowicz (1995, 1997) in Hong Kong showed supervisors reported students had difficulties with surface-level grammar, but that these difficulties were not as important as difficulties affecting the expression of ideas. A further study in the US (Dong, 1998) found that ESL postgraduate students experienced particular difficulty with the sequencing and development of ideas. Studies (such as, Cooley and Lewkowicz, 1995, 1997; Dong, 1998; Thompson, 1999) indicated that student writers found it difficult to structure an argument over an extended stretch of discourse. Further studies indicated that students struggled to understand what content to include in individual chapters and how it should be organized (Bitchener and Basturkmen, 2006). Last but not least, the teacher considered the difficulties his own students had in understanding the 'content and organizational requirements' for the various sections of the thesis and in articulating ideas and information using suitably 'academic' forms of expression.

The teacher also examined 'research methodology' courses offered in the local context and found that the courses did not focus specifically on the particular needs (needs related to the content and organizational requirements for sections of the thesis and academic forms of expression) he had considered. The research methodology courses focused largely on the research process rather than the kind of micro elements in the sections of the thesis that were to constitute the major focus of the workshop series.

In summary, this was an unusual needs analysis situation – the class was quite diverse and the class members were not fixed. In an effort to understand needs, the teacher in this case drew on a number of sources of information. He discussed needs informally with colleagues (other supervisors) and students. He drew on the research literature, which, given his own research interests in the area, was a literature with which he was very familiar. He drew also on his own experiences as a supervisor of masters and doctoral students.

8.3   Investigating specialist discourse

The investigation of discourse was based on a genre-analytical approach. Each section or chapter (for example, abstract, introduction, literature review, discussion of results) was considered one at a time. (See Chapter 3 for an overview of genre analysis as a method of inquiry.) The teacher drew on the genre-based descriptions of parts of the thesis in the burgeoning research literature and on his own research in the area. The latter had led him to collect sample chapters and consider them in terms of their functions, areas of content, organization and linguistic features (features of use or language expression). The approach and findings of this investigation is illustrated below in reference to the discussion of results. (In some theses the 'Discussion of Results' is a separate chapter but in some it is a section in the 'Results' chapter. The remainder of this chapter uses the term 'Discussion of Results' chapter to refer to either possibility.)

8.3.1   Functions, content and organization

From the literature and his research, the teacher has produced a description of the functions, content and organization typically found in the Discussion of Results. The chapter functions to review the aims of the research, the theoretical basis for the study and the methodological approach and to discuss the contribution of the study to the field and to interpret, explain and evaluate the results. In line with genre-based descriptions generally, the organization is described in terms of moves. Figure 8.1 shows a representation of moves in the Discussion of Results. The moves show the type of content and organization typically involved. The moves can be recycled and indicate the options available to the writers.

8.3.2   Linguistic features

Whereas the teacher's first strand of investigation was broad in focus – an attempt to account for macro features (functions, content and organization) – the second

Moves

1. Provide background information
   Sub moves
      Restatement of:
      a. aims, research questions and hypotheses
      b. key published research
      c. research/methodological approach

2. Present a statement of result
   Sub moves
      a. restatement of a key result
      b. expanded statement about a key result

3. Evaluate/comment on results
   Sub moves
      a. explanation of result – suggest reasons for result
      b. comment on whether it was an expected or unexpected result
      c. reference to compare result to previously published research
      d. provide examples of result
      e. make a general claim on the basis on the result, for example, drawing a conclusion or stating a hypothesis
      f. quote previous research to support the claim
      g. make suggestion for future research
      h. explain why further research is needed

Figure 8.1   Content and organization of the Discussion of Results
Source: Based on Bitchener (2010), p. 180

strand had a narrow focus on what the teacher describes as 'micro' issues of language use and expression. The aim was to identify salient linguistic features in the various sections or chapters of the thesis. For example, as shown in Figure 8.1, the Discussion of Results is the section in which writers typically make general claims based on their results. The conviction writers feel towards these claims can vary. The writer may feel some claims are clearly justified whereas others are less clearly so. The writer will thus wish to make some claims assertively. The writer will wish to make other claims tentatively in order to indicate that this is only one possible explanation or conclusion. Investigation shows that in signalling their conviction or lack of it, writers use 'hedges', a type of a discourse marker, to indicate how much certainty the writer has in the claim being made. Figure 8.2 shows some of the hedges used in a sample masters thesis that was investigated.

The reader will recall that genre analysis was one of the approaches to investigating specialist discourse reviewed earlier in this work (Chapter 3), and that the approach can involve 'text analysis' alone (samples of the genre or genres of interest are examined for their typical patterns and features) or 'text analysis' along with ethnographic inquiry into how the discourse community that produces the genre(s) perceives its or their roles, functions and values. This combination of text analysis and ethnographic inquiry was used in the present case. The teacher/course developer conducted interviews with academic staff members who were supervising students and the students themselves in an endeavour to find out

Assertive claim

The results of the current study do not support this conclusion (the conclusion in a previously published study).

The use of 'do not support' presents a clear and direct message or statement of 'fact'.

Tentative

The findings above seemed to reveal the dual character of ...
It is possible, however, that the learners' behaviour in the class context was influenced by ...

The use of 'seemed to' and 'it is possible' indicate the writer wishes to show a lack of certainty about the claims being made.

Figure 8.2   Examples of hedges
Source: Adapted from Bitchener (2010), pp. 192–3

their understandings of the various sections or chapters of the thesis. For example, the teacher/course developer drew on an inquiry (Bitchener and Basturkmen, 2006; Basturkmen and Bitchener, 2005) in which supervisors and their students were asked to discuss samples of the students' writing of the discussion of results sections. The students were at the stage of writing up their thesis. They had already submitted a draft of Discussions of Results and they brought copies of these drafts to the interviews to refer to. The inquiry aimed to find out what the supervisors and students saw as the role and functions of this chapter, what they expected it to contain and their perceptions of students' difficulties in writing it. (A further aim was to see if supervisors and the students they were supervising shared the same perspectives.) The difficulties the supervisors identified revealed their 'criteria' for evaluating writing in this chapter and thus the values they held for it. Figure 8.3 shows some of the interview questions for supervisors.

The supervisors identified three broad functions of the Discussion of Results chapter: it should summarize the results, discuss the results and make links between the results of the present study and the literature. Their responses to the interview questions also provided insights into their views of the functions at a more in-depth level. An excerpt from one of the interviews is shown on the following page. In the excerpt, the supervisor describes a relationship between two of the broad functions: the writer can discuss a result by relating it to an explanation in the literature. The excerpt also shows the supervisor's perspective on a difficulty that students may have:

> Students don't know the purpose of this section and find it difficult to link the content of the study back to the literature. Instead they tend to think THEY have to come up with explanations of their results.

In sum, the investigation of specialist discourse was a genre-based inquiry into moves and their linguistic features in the various parts and chapters of the thesis. Given that there is a considerable body of literature on this topic, the

In this interview I would like to ask some questions about your students' writing of theses. I am interested in difficulties you may perceive in the writing of the Discussion of Results section in particular.

I would like to ask you some general questions:

Can you tell me about any difficulties you have noticed in the writing of the Discussion of Results sections of the students you supervise?

Now I would like to ask you about some specific types of possible difficulties:

Have you noticed difficulties in:

understanding the functions of the Discussion of Results?

selecting content?

organizing content?

showing appropriate stance (how writers position themselves)?

grammar and word choice ? (Can you give an example or two?)

Which of these possible areas do you think are the most important?

Finally, I would like to ask you about the writing of (name of one student).

What, if any, do you see as this student's main problems?

Could you show me samples of these problems in the student's writing?

Figure 8.3   Interview questions for supervisors
Source: Adapted from Bitchener and Basturkmen (2006)

teacher/course developer in this case drew on this literature as well as conducting his own investigation. The investigation was text based in the sense that sample chapters and sections were examined for their typical patterns of organization and salient linguistic features. It was supplemented with an ethnographic inquiry into the perceptions of the academic discourse community in the local context.

8.4   Designing the workshop series and materials

A five-part workshop series was devised. The workshops are held and re-held over the course of the academic year, generally during the weekends. As described above, the workshops are 'open access' and students attend whichever and as many workshops as they wish. The workshop series is not credit bearing and does not involve course work or assignments for the students.

The series covers all the parts and chapters of the thesis (abstract, introduction, literature review, and so forth). The first two workshops are extensive events that begin at 9 a.m. and finish at 3 p.m. As shown in Figure 8.4, these workshops focus on a number of parts or chapters of the thesis (each part or chapter is dealt with individually). The third workshop is a four-hour workshop focusing entirely on the literature review. The remaining two workshops focus on 'genres' of writing leading into and following on from the thesis (the proposal and the research-based article respectively). Some students elect to attend only some workshops or parts of them (depending on the stage they

Workshop 1

This is the first of a two-part weekend workshop to introduce students to the various chapters and sections of a thesis including the abstract, introduction and literature review. The workshop will provide you with opportunities to interact orally in both small groups and as a plenary group. Sample extracts from excellent theses will be used to illustrate the material that is presented.

Workshop 2

This workshop is a follow on from Weekend Workshop 1 and will cover the thesis methodology, presentation and discussion of results, and the conclusion.

Workshop 3: Preparing for and writing your literature review

This 4-hour workshop will focus on defining the scope of the review, researching and preparing to write the review, organizing and structuring the material, and writing drafts of the review. The session will be interactive. Sample materials will be critiqued.

Workshop 4: From thesis to article

This workshop focuses on the process involved in writing an article based on data from a thesis. The workshop looks at (1) choosing an appropriate topic and focus, (2) the structure and language of an article, (3) choosing an appropriate journal, (4) what editors focus on when deciding if a manuscript is suitable for publication, and (5) stages in the submission process. Textual examples will be discussed during the interactive seminar.

Workshop 5: Launching the thesis and writing the thesis proposal

This 2-hour seminar will focus on the issues that students need to consider when deciding on the area of research that will be investigated for a thesis (the field of investigation, the literature search, identifying a research gap, framing research questions, determining an appropriate design and methodology) and writing the research proposal. Instruction and sample analyses will be provided.

Figure 8.4   Workshop series: Outline of content

have reached in their writing up or depending on the chapter or part they feel is difficult for them) while other students attend the whole series in order to get an overview of the entire body of content.

The approach to instruction is largely genre-based. It involves teacher-led description and discussion and this is interspersed with pair and small group work in 'text analysis' and discussion tasks. A session may begin with teacher-led discussion of the functions of the chapter or part, followed by an overview of the typical content and organization involved in it. The latter generally takes the form of a presentation of move sequence (based on the literature). The teacher leads a discussion of a text sample (taken from theses that have been evaluated as particularly well written according to conventional academic standards and expectations). Further text samples are provided and students working in pairs or small groups analyse these for the moves that have been described earlier to see the extent to which the writer in question has drawn on the moves and which options he or she has and has not drawn on in particular. This is followed by a focus on linguistic features. A similar format is followed – the teacher identifies and describes the feature(s), leads the class in examining a sample text and the class breaks into pair and small groups to analyse the linguistic features in further texts samples. The whole class reconvenes to discuss their findings and to discuss what they have observed in research writing in their own disciplines in terms of similarities and possible differences with the description and examples used in the workshop.

Figure 8.5 shows a small part of the material developed for the literature review workshop. Section A provides an overview of the functions of the literature review and Section B an overview of its general organization. Section C offers a description of the options (the moves writers variously select) and provides a text sample analysed for the moves. The sentences in the sample have been numbered for the purposes of discussion. Section D lists the criteria for evaluating literature reviews. Section E focuses on linguistic elements. Section F discusses the 'frequently asked questions' students ask.

8.5   Responding to difficulties and constraints

The teacher/course developer in the present case identified 'time' as the particular constraint that hindered the development of the workshop series. In this case, it was not a lack of time on the part of the teacher but lack of time on the part of the students that led to limitations on the types of teaching activities that could be used. Since the students contemporaneously take subject courses (in some cases), carry out their research study (in most cases), write up their research and work as well (in many cases), it is understandable that they feel they can give only very limited time to the topic of 'writing the thesis'. And yet they want to know how to go about what is in most cases the most complex piece of writing that they have so far undertaken. The limitations of time have resulted in the teacher opting for a mainly 'deductive' approach. The term 'deductive' is used here to refer to an approach in which the model/description is presented first and the students then study examples and/or apply it to analysis of examples. This can be contrasted to an 'inductive' approach in which the students begin by examining examples/samples (of text) before the model is presented and a variant of this ('guided discovery') in which students themselves 'discover' patterns (moves or linguistics features in this case) in the text samples. However, given that the students are short of time and given also that only few are from language and communication disciplinary areas (thus might be expected to have an intrinsic interest in language use), the teacher opted for what he described as a 'giving them the information straight' strategy (a deductive approach) despite his own preferences as an educator.

The students' lack of time combined with the fact that the workshop series is not a 'course' (students are not required to do assignments and are not graded) has meant that the students do not 'do writing' in the workshops. The focus of the workshops is limited to descriptions of writing but does not include actual

132

A
Functions of a thesis literature review

1. A review of the **non-research literature** that summarizes and synthesizes background and contextual information.
2. A review of **theoretical perspectives** that underpin or inform your research project.
3. A review of the **research literature** relevant to your study.
4. a **critique** that
   (a) identifies arguments for and against issues and controversies related to functions 1–3 above and
   (b) assesses or weighs up the value of theories, ideas, claims, research designs, methods and conclusions, including an identification of strengths and weaknesses.
5. An identification of **gaps or shortcomings** in this knowledge and research.
6. A **rationale** justifying why the gap was important and significant enough to be filled.
7. An explanation of **how the design and execution of your research project was informed** by steps 1–6 above. This is likely to explain how the literature provided
   (a) a focus for the research questions or hypotheses that were investigated and
   (b) guidelines for an appropriate methodology and design.

B
Organizational options for a literature review

1. the themes and topics of the review
2. the research questions or hypotheses being addressed
3. the variables investigated in the study
4. a chronological presentation of non-research and research literature
5. a combination of these options

C
Main move and sub-move options

Moves	Sub-moves
1. Establish some aspect of the knowledge territory relevant to your research.	a. A presentation of knowledge claims and statements about theories, beliefs, constructs, definitions.
	b. A statement about the centrality, importance or significance of the theme/topic.
	c. A presentation of research evidence (e.g. findings, methodology).
2. Create a research niche/gap in knowledge.	a. A critique of knowledge claims, issues, problems associated with move 1 claims/statements.
	b. A presentation of research evidence in relation to move 2a.
	c. An identification of gap(s) in knowledge and/or research.
	d. A continuation or development of a tradition that has been established but not fully investigated.
	e. A presentation of arguments for introducing a new perspective or theoretical framework (as a result of move 1 claims/statement).

Figure 8.5 Sample material from the literature review workshop
Note: The material in Figure 8.5 was developed for the workshop series and has subsequently been published in a book (Bitchener, 2010).

3. Announce how you will occupy the research niche/gap.	a. An announcement of the aim of the research study.
	b. An announcement of the theoretical position(s) or framework(s).
	c. An announcement of the research design and processes.
	d. An announcement of how you define concepts and terms in your research.

Example

1. One measure, a willingness to communicate scale, developed by McCroskey and Richmond, attempted to assess 'a personality-based, trait-like predisposition which is relatively consistent across a variety of communication contexts and any types of receivers' (1987: 5).	Move 1a (claim)
2. The scale was intended to measure the extent to which a person was willing to communicate and it included items related to four communication contexts – public speaking, talking at meetings, talking in small groups and talking in dyads with three types of receivers – strangers, acquaintances and friends.	Move 1c (evidence)
3. Results of studies using the WTC scale (McCroskey and Baer 1985; McCroskey and McCroskey 1986a, b) suggested that an individual willing to communicate in one context with one receiver type was highly correlated with willingness to communicate in other contexts and with other receiver types.	Moves 1a, 1c (claim & evidence)
4. This did not mean, however, that an individual was equally willing to communicate in all contexts and with all types of receivers, and research directed at considering the relationship generally found that the larger the number of receivers, and the more distant the relationship between the individual and the receiver(s), the less willing an individual was to communicate (McCroskey and Richmond 1991; McCroskey 1992).	Move 1a (claim) Move 1c (evidence)
5. Yet the WTC scale appeared to offer the best instrument, for reliability and validity, in measuring the WTC construct (McCroskey and Richmond 1987).	Move 1a (claim) Move 1c (evidence)
6. Studies conducted in the United States found high levels of reliability; and furthermore, reliability estimates generated from both western and eastern cultures (in L1) appeared to be consistent with those obtained in the United States (McCroskey 1992, Asker 1998).	
7. In addition, a number of research studies provided some support for its construct and content validity.	
8. McCroskey (1992: 21) concluded that the assumptions underlying the WTC instrument were tenable and that the content validity appeared to be satisfactory.	
9. Similarly, Asker (1998: 166) claimed that the content validity of the data in his study seemed to be satisfactory and consistent with findings from other studies.	
Extract from Cao, K. 2006. 'Willingness to Communicate in the Second Language Classroom', MA thesis, University of Auckland.	

Figure 8.5 Continued

D
Research literature evaluation questions (selection)

1. Is the research issue clearly stated?
2. Is its context sufficiently explained?
3. Is there sufficient justification for the research?
4. Are the research questions/hypotheses clearly framed?
5. Is the methodological approach relevant and comprehensive enough for these questions/hypotheses?
6. Are the methods of data collection appropriate and sufficiently wide ranging to produce satisfactory answers?
7. Are the research instruments appropriate for the research?
8. Are the variables and constructs of the research clearly defined and scoped?
9. Are the data collection procedures sufficiently complete?
10. Are the data analysis procedures appropriate?

E
Linguistic strategies for evaluating published literature (selection)

Strategies	Purpose	Examples
Hedges	To withhold your full commitment to a statement	*May; might; possibly; likely; seemed to; appeared to*
Boosters	To reveal your certainty about a statement	*Clearly; definitely; without doubt*
Attitude markers	To reveal your attitude towards a statement	*Interestingly; surprisingly; unfortunately*
Engagement markers	To build a relationship with the reader	*As you can see; you will have noted that; consider whether*

F
Frequently asked questions (selection)

How do I decide what to include and what not to include in the literature review?

The advice I give my students is that the research questions/hypotheses must guide you in determining what is/is not relevant. You can ask yourself the following questions:

(1) Which aspect of my thesis does this literature relate to?
(2) Does it add anything new to what has been included already?

Following the mind-map approach introduced earlier in this chapter should help you decide whether or not a certain piece of literature is relevant.

Should I refer to methodology literature in my literature review?

The literature informing your own methodology is usually presented in the methodology chapter. However, when you are reviewing and evaluating your literature review material, you may refer to various aspects of methodology in order to explain why a claim or a finding, for example, is or is not valid and convincing. Sometimes, and this is more likely to be the case for a doctoral thesis, a separate literature review chapter focuses on methodological issues alone.

If many writers/researchers have made the same claim, how many should I refer to?

Generally speaking, you would be best to refer to three or four, making sure that you include the most recent and the most significant. Concerning the latter, you would certainly want to include an earlier seminal work.

Figure 8.5 Continued

writing tasks. Ideally, the teacher would like the workshop series to become a credit-bearing course and to involve writing tasks in which students 'transfer' what they having been learning about (for example, move sequence in a section of the thesis) to writing a segment of their thesis. The latter would involve the students in using content from research and working in pairs or small groups of students from the same discipline to provide peer review of the writing.

The teacher would like to assess learning. The instruction provided in the workshops aims to help students develop an awareness of the generic features of the thesis but how do students apply this awareness when it comes to their own writing? At present the students do not carry out written assignments and so evidence that the approach is effective has relied largely (although not completely) on students' comments in workshop evaluations. (See Cheng (2006) for a review of studies indicating the effectiveness of genre-based ESP instruction.) It is possible that the workshop series will be reconfigured in the future into a 'course' structure that would allow for the kinds of developments described above.

8.6 Summary

The workshop series described in this chapter illustrates a programme that not only had to respond to the possibility that the 'needs' of the students were diverse (students from diverse disciplines and who were at different stages of their research) but also had to respond to a particularly challenging set of 'real world' constraints (limited time on the part of the students, the fact that the students were not required to attend, complete assignments or be assessed). As we have seen, these challenges led to the design of a flexible, open-access programme.

In devising the content for the workshops, the teacher worked to transform information from a well-established research literature and his own research in the area (research into, for example, descriptions of the parts of the thesis, linguistic features of academic writing and the writing difficulties of non-native speaking students) into a 'time effective format' for teaching purposes. The workshops aimed to help students 'see' the typical content and organization of chapters and parts of a thesis, an underlying structure which all too often is not apparent to the untrained eye and thus help them in organizing parts and chapters in their own theses. It also aimed to help them 'notice' linguistic features in the parts and chapters. It is also hoped that the students can transfer the 'genre analytical' skills they develop in the thesis writing workshop series to other genres they encounter.

8.7 Discussion

1. How would you classify the English for Thesis Writing workshop series in relation to the categorizations shown in Figure 1.1 (Areas of ESP Teaching) and Figure 1.2 (Time of Course in Relation to Experience)?

2. Where would you situate the series on the wide- and narrow-angled continuum discussed in Chapter 4?

3. Much of the instruction in the workshops drew on a genre-based approach. In this approach the students are helped to perceive the patterns and features underlying the genre(s) of interest and apply this understanding to the analysis of sample texts and in writing their own text. Hyland (2003) describes genre-based writing instruction as often initially teacher-led, centred on analysis of model texts and explicit attention to form, a visible pedagogy enabling students to see clearly what is to be learnt and how it will be assessed. Have you had experience in teaching or learning writing using a genre-based approach and, if so, what do you see as its advantages? Are there potentially any drawbacks?

4. In the present case, the teacher/course developer was a member of the academic discourse community and was familiar with the practices of the genres (the sections and chapters of the thesis) and the values held for them by the academic discourse community. But what if the ESP teacher/course developer is not a member of discourse community in question? How much can the ESP teacher be expected to know about a genre unless she or he is a member of the discourse community that produces and reproduces the genre? How might the ESP teacher/course developer investigate the practice and values held for a genre in a discourse community with which he or she is not familiar? What role might ethnographic inquiry play? Which 'ethnographic' means of inquiry used in the present case could the teacher draw on and can you suggest any further means to understand the role of a genre in an unfamiliar discourse community?

5. Although parts and chapters of a thesis may share common ground across disciplines, they may vary to some extent. How could you use the representation of moves in the discussion section shown in Figure 8.1 to investigate writing in two or more different disciplines?

Acknowledgements

I express my gratitude to Professor John Bitchener of AUT University, Auckland for allowing me to examine the Genre Writing Workshop Series for the purposes of the case study described in this chapter. Some materials from the series are published in Bitchener (2010).

9
Conclusion

This book has been divided into two parts. Part I introduced and discussed three important areas in ESP course development: analysing needs, investigating specialist discourse and determining the curriculum. The chapters introduced the options possible for analysing needs (for example, interviews, questionnaires and observations), investigating specialist discourse (for example, ethnography, corpus and genre analytical approaches) and determining the curriculum (for example, wide- and narrow-angled course designs). To an extent, the discussion in Part I was hypothetical – what ESP teachers/course developers *can* do.

Part II introduced and discussed four case studies (Case 1, Case 2, Case 3 and Case 4). Each case reported the development of an ESP course for a distinct group of learners and the particular challenges this posed for the teacher(s)/course developer(s) in question. The chapters in Part II examined how the teacher(s)/course developer(s) went about investigating needs and specialist discourse and determining the curriculum in a particular context. The focus of these chapters was on the decisions the teachers/course developers made in response to the realities of the given situation. Whereas Part I was somewhat abstract (the *possible* options), Part II was more concrete – the *actual* decisions the teachers made in developing their courses.

This concluding chapter is organized into three sections. The first section revisits the topics of needs analysis, investigation of specialist discourse and determining the curriculum and asks what can be learnt from the case studies in general. In other words, how can practice inform theory? The second section provides a visual representation of ESP course development. The third and final section considers trends in this field.

9.1   Revisiting the main considerations in ESP course development

9.1.1   Needs analysis

Needs analysis has long been argued to be the cornerstone of ESP and the case studies examined in this work lend support to the centrality of needs analysis in the development of ESP courses. In all four cases, the primacy of needs was clearly evident. It was what the learners 'needed' that determined the features of discourse and the types of texts that were investigated. It was on the basis of these needs that the ESP courses were constructed. It was an understanding of what the learners needed that paved the way for the great majority of the course design decisions.

Finding out very clearly those aspects of language use and communication in the target situation that were problematic for the students was an important concern for the teachers/course developers in all the cases. This mostly involved a one-step investigation. However, in Case 1 (English for Police) it involved two steps. In this case, the teachers knew very little about police work at the outset of the preparation of the course. They first needed to identify the areas of work and the language-based real-world tasks the prospective police recruits would be engaged in before they could start work on identifying the tasks the students had difficulty in. However, in the other three cases the analysis was a one-stage rather than two-stage process. In these cases, the work or study areas and tasks were a 'given'. For example, it was already known that an important area of work for the overseas-trained medical doctors in Case 2 was the 'medical consultation' and it was already known that organizing a literature chapter was a critical task for the postgraduate research students in Case 4. The teachers in these three cases could directly focus their investigation on identification of the language-based tasks the students found difficult and the features of language use, genres and skills they needed for effective communication in them. The needs analysis literature has generally represented target situation analysis as a single step but this review suggests that sometimes it involves two steps: the first stage to map out the areas and real-world tasks in the target situation and the second stage to identify the linguistic demands and difficulties associated with those tasks.

Furthermore, in general the literature has distinguished between target situation analysis (what the students need to do) and present situation (or deficiency) analysis (what the students can or cannot do in relation to those needs) (see Chapter 2). This distinction may give the impression that these are two sequential elements (first describe language needs in the target situation and then identify which of these are difficult for the students). But as we have seen, the overriding concern of the course developers in the case studies was to investigate student difficulties. Thus they did not focus on 'what students need to do' unless it was understood to be a 'difficulty' for the students. So although the medical doctors in Case 2 obviously needed good listening skills for the medical consultations, since this was not generally an area of difficulty it was closed down as an area of investigation. The teachers in the case studies were largely concerned with *investigating their students' language difficulties in work or study tasks*. Target situation and present situation analysis can therefore be seen as two sides of the same coin.

The experienced teachers in the case studies gathered information on needs from multiple sources and perspectives (unlike the teachers in some of the hypothetical scenarios in Chapter 2). The choice of who to consult and procedures to gather information depended on the exigencies of the situation in question. For example, in analysing the needs of the police officers in Case 1, the teachers went out 'on patrol' and in investigating needs in Case 2, the teacher observed overseas-trained doctors in role play medical consultations with their 'actor' patients. Among other means of collecting information there was the collection of lecturers' feedback on written scripts in Case 3 and discussions with research supervisors in Case 4.

The English for Visual Arts course was the only one of the courses that targeted pre-experience students. The teacher in this case came to the conclusion that the course needed to focus on conceptual (disciplinary) content as well as language. This may suggest a link between needs analysis and the timing of a course in relation to the experience of the students (see Figure 1.2). If the students do not have prior experience, ESP teachers/course developers are more likely to investigate conceptual needs as well as language needs. If students are during- or post-experience, the teacher may assume the students have already developed this conceptual base.

The teachers' interests and theories appeared to influence the investigations of needs in the case studies. Examples include the teacher in Case 4 who espoused genre theory and investigated needs from this perspective and the teachers in Case 1 whose expertise in corpus-based techniques enabled them to conduct their investigation from corpus-linguistic perspectives. As Robinson (1991) has argued:

> The needs that are established for a particular group of students will be an outcome of a needs analysis project and will be influenced by ideological preconceptions of the analysts. A different group of analysts working with the same group of students, but with different views on teaching and learning, would be highly likely to produce a different set of needs. (p. 7)

Pursuing a similar line of thought, Hyland (2008, p. 113) has argued that needs analysis like other classroom practices involves decisions that are based on the teachers' interests, values and beliefs about language, learning and teaching. As argued before in this work, and as seen in the case studies, needs analysis is not an entirely procedural endeavour. It is not just a matter of technicalities but of theoretical perspectives as well.

9.1.2 Investigating specialist discourse

The review of case studies has shown the lengths to which the teachers/course developers went and the varied means they used to investigate specialist discourse, especially aspects of the discourse presenting difficulties for their students. As we have seen, the teachers investigated the target communities' expectations and values for genres and types of spoken interactions as well as written and spoken texts (the samples of written and spoken discourse). For example, the teachers/course developers in Case 1 (police) endeavoured to find out what senior police officers expected of genres and interactions used in policing and the teacher in Case 3 (visual arts) examined assignments that Arts lecturers had rated highly.

The teachers/course developers drew on a range of approaches to investigate discourse. However, in investigations of *written discourse*, all the course developers drew on genre analysis, thus providing evidence for the predominance of this approach in ESP-oriented discourse analysis.

All the cases involved an ethnographic thrust of inquiry. For the teachers in the first two cases this resulted in quite extensive periods of fieldwork, especially observations of spoken interactions in the target situations ('ride-alongs' with the police and 'sitting in' on general practice clinics). The role of 'insider informants' (members of the target communities of practice) was critical for investigation of discourse in all four cases. None of the teachers/course developers attempted to work in isolation without consulting informants, such as research supervisors in Case 4 and the professional development trainers in Case 2.

Chapter 3 suggested course developers should search for any existing data and descriptions before generating and analysing their own data. It was suggested that course developers make use of and build on information already available in their investigations of specialist discourse. It was argued that there is often no need to 'reinvent the wheel'. The reader may recall the hypothetical example of the university teacher (Chapter 3) who in developing an academic listening-skills course proceeded by collecting (with a great deal of time and effort) recordings of lectures in his local context, transcribing the lectures and identifying markers of topic change in them (the students had found it difficult to follow topic development in lectures). He had proceeded in this way although published research on topic change in lectures and corpora of lectures in comparable settings were available. But, as the case of the course for medical doctors has shown, these suggestions are not always relevant. The investigation of discourse in Case 2 focused on the ways of communicating in a specific regional context and medical community and inquired into idiomatic word choices and local ways of expressing medical concerns since it was precisely these aspects of the medical consultation that were difficult for a number of the overseas-trained doctors. Although the teacher/course developer was aware of the research and publications in the area of discourse in medical consultations, she could make only limited use of these sources. Instead, she needed to find sources of data from local contexts.

Detailed, accurate and realistic descriptions of language use are needed in developing courses in ESP (see Chapter 3). The cases have shown a range of means by which the teachers set about producing or identifying such descriptions.

9.1.3   Determining the curriculum

Chapter 4 examined distinctions between wide- and narrow-angled course designs and argued that 'wide' and 'narrow' can usefully be seen as two ends of a continuum rather than as *either* and *or*. The courses described in the case studies were mainly towards the 'narrow' end of this continuum. None were at the very end of this continuum, and arguably this was because the courses focused on the immediate and shared needs of the course participants. The course in Case 1 focused on the immediate needs of the prospective police officers. Although these officers may eventually enter different branches of police work (for example, traffic or community policing), the ESP course was devised to reflect needs and discourse in an amalgam of the branches. Similarly, the course in Case 2 focused on the shared and immediate needs of the medical doctors to pass a component of the registration exam. The doctors' long-term language needs may vary should the doctors pursue various specializations later on.

Turning to the EAP case studies, the course for visual arts students illustrates a narrow-angled course targeting the needs of learners in one particular discipline (ESAP). The English for Thesis Writing course in Chapter 8 focused on the needs of learners across disciplines (EGAP). Chapter 4 reviewed theoretical arguments for narrow-angled, ESAP, course designs. Discourse communities, it was argued, vary not only in regard to their communicative practices (such as, the genres they produce) but also in their perspectives of what information is important and how they form their arguments. Sometimes decisions on this topic (wide- or narrow-angled course designs) are as contingent on the exigencies of the situation as theoretical concerns. In Case 4, the motivation for the thesis-writing course arose from the needs expressed by students and supervisors from a range of disciplines. In short, the way a course is focused in regard to the wide and narrow continuum appears at least in part determined by the situation in which the course emerges.

Generally, specificity in ESP course design has been construed in terms of whether the course targets needs for one particular discipline or work area. However, specificity can also be related to the aims of the course. The course for the medical doctors focused on language and communication in one very specific event (the patient-centred medical consultation) whereas the course for police focused on a number of events and genres in policing. The course for thesis writers, although concerned with the needs of students across disciplines, was highly specific in that it focused on one communicative event (the thesis). Thus I would argue that 'specificity' in ESP course design is not only related to whether the course focuses on the needs of learners in one particular work or study area. Courses can be narrow angled in terms of the focus of instruction: they can be focused narrowly on one genre or type of interaction, such as, the patient-centred consultation and the thesis genre, or they can be focused more widely on a range of sections of the thesis and interactions in the target situation.

The case study teachers/course developers all produced their own teaching materials and used authentic written and spoken texts from the target communities widely in this. For example, written texts were used to illustrate the form and content of particular sections of the thesis in Case 4. It was noticeable that tasks embedded in the teaching materials appeared to be related to activities associated with the specific work or study area. Examples of this were the 'investigative' tasks in using the web-based corpus materials in Case 1 (police), the 'observation' of video recordings in Case 2 (doctors) and the text 'analytical' tasks in Case 4 (research students). In the interviews that were part of the preparation for the case studies, none of the teachers/course developers raised this point. This relationship did not seem to be an aspect of course development they consciously attended to. However, the 'fit' between the pedagogical tasks they developed and activity types associated with work and study areas suggested that at some level the teachers did 'make use of the underlying methodology and the activities of the discipline it serves' (Dudley-Evans and St John, 1998, pp. 4–5).

The course syllabuses involved a range of content areas including communication skills, genres, disciplinary concepts and discourse features. 'Writing' content largely consisted of genres and 'speaking' content consisted of communication skills and features of spoken discourse. The courses did not to any great extent focus on technical terms in the specific fields. In fact, the course for medical doctors targeted the everyday, non-technical expressions for health concerns that are used by laypeople rather than medical terminology. This reflected the needs of the students; the doctors already knew the medical terminology. Across the courses, vocabulary materials predominantly targeted multi-word items (lexical phrases, conventional expressions and collocations) rather than single word items. This again reflected the teachers' understanding of their students' needs.

It is generally understood that ESP aims to help students meet the linguistic requirements of the community of practice or discipline they wish to enter or make progress in. Not surprisingly therefore, the teachers/course developers in the case studies referred to standards and performance criteria of those communities and disciplinary members for evaluating learning. Thus, in the case of the course for medical doctors, the teacher drew on the criteria for the patient-centred consultation as set out by the professional development trainers who were members of the local medical community (see Figures 6.2 and 6.4).

9.2   A visual representation of ESP course development

A representation of ESP course development is set out in Figure 9.1. The figure shows the three areas of ESP course development examined in this work

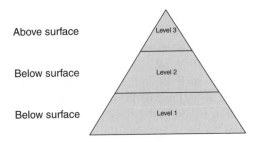

Above surface

Below surface

Below surface

Level 1: Analysing needs

Considerations

Situation analysis: What tasks are involved in the work or study area and what are the standards for their performance? Can the tasks be divided into subtasks?

What type of needs to investigate (for example, objective and/or subjective, immediate/long term, skills and/or tasks)?

Which language-based skills or tasks do the students find difficult?

What is the nature of the students' difficulties in these language-based skills or tasks (for example, linguistic, conceptual, cultural)?

****

Level 2: Investigating specialist discourse

Considerations

Which linguistic forms and features to investigate (for example, those the students are weak in or unaware of, those members of the community of practice stress as important)?

What data to collect (for example, do relevant literature, descriptions and corpora already exist or does primary data need to be collected)?

What approach to use in the investigation (for example, ethnography and/or text analysis)?

What primary data to collect (texts, marked scripts of students' writing, observations, self-reports, such as interviews)?

How to analyse the texts/discourse from the target community of practice or discipline (for example, whole or part of the texts, for specific features)?

How to devise pedagogical descriptions of discourse in the specialist area?

****

Level 3: Determining the curriculum

Considerations

How to focus of the course (for example, wide- or narrow-angled)

How to deliver the course (for example, web-based, classes, workshops, on-site or off-site)?

What units to include in the syllabus and how to sequence them (for example, genres, features of spoken discourse, conceptual content, easy to difficult, immediate to less immediate needs)?

How to evaluate learning (for example, with reference to the final or way-stage criteria or performance objectives used in the community of practice)?

What materials to develop and what types of tasks to include (for example, pedagogical descriptions of discourse and tasks that make use of activities of the work or study area)?

Figure 9.1 Representation of ESP course development

(analysing needs, investigating specialist discourse and determining the curriculum) and the relationship between them. It also shows some of the considerations teachers and course developers make in each area.

The representation is in the form of a pyramid to signify that ESP courses (the curriculum and materials) are built on the foundations of investigations of needs and specialist discourse. Since findings from these investigations underpin many of the decisions made in regard to the curriculum and materials, the pyramid is a multi-level structure. Needs analysis and investigations of specialist discourse are the 'below the surface' levels. Findings from needs analysis are the bedrock. These findings indicate the aspects of discourse or genres the course developer can usefully investigate (usually those that the students have difficulty with). The considerable efforts of course developers at the first two levels are the 'spade work' forming the basis for the development of the curriculum. The curriculum is the surface-level structure, the visible element. The curriculum rests on the foundations of needs analysis and investigation of specialist discourse.

9.3　Future trends

Thus far this chapter looked back and revisited core areas of ESP course development. This final section looks forward at the trends in this field. The review of literature and the case studies show that to date needs analysis has largely been construed as an activity for the teacher/course developer, and as an activity in which students are 'investigated'. But could students participate in this activity? Holme and Chalauisaeng (2006) suggest this may be possible. These writers report on a method of 'participatory appraisal' devised to encourage students to act as investigators of their own needs.

In recent years, needs analysts have increasingly used tasks as the focus of inquiry (Long, 2005; Cowling, 2007; Thomas, 2009). Tasks are units not defined by linguistic criteria and task-based needs analyses aim to identify the 'real world' work or study tasks in the target situation. For example, Thomas' (2009) task-based needs analysis in a civil engineering company found that 'applying for a building consent' was a key task and that the engineers broke this complex task down into a set of subtasks. It is expected that this trend will continue and that analysts will continue to seek to identify the language-based tasks involved in the work or study area of interest, which of these the students find difficult and the nature of student difficulties in them.

In addition, it is expected that the kinds of ethnographic methods (observations, interviews, fieldwork) used to investigate specialist discourse that have been described in this work will continue. There is growing recognition that text analysis alone is insufficient for the investigation of specialist discourse. Text analysis can show the patterns and regularities in discourse but it cannot explain why the texts are produced in the ways they are. Thus there has been a move towards attempting to understand what text regularities reveal about the ways of thinking of the communities of practice and disciplines. This trend will continue and more ESP-oriented investigations will focus on *explaining* specialist language use as well as *describing* it.

9.4 Summary

This book has examined three key areas of ESP course development, needs analysis, investigating specialist discourse and determining the ESP curriculum. The chapters in Part I provided an overview of literature in these areas. The chapters in Part II described case studies in ESP course development. This concluding chapter brought the two parts together to discuss insights from the case studies in relation to the concepts described in the chapters in Part I. The chapter *built* on concepts from the literature and the review of case studies to provide a visual representation of ESP course development. The representation showed how the three areas of course development are related and the kinds of considerations teachers and course developers make in each area. The representation was in the form of a structure, a pyramid, to convey the idea that much of the work in ESP course development is taken up with building the foundations (through the analysis of needs and specialist discourse). And finally, the chapter identified trends in the area of ESP course development.

References

Abbuhl, R. J. (2005) *The Effect of Feedback and Instruction on Writing Quality: Legal Writing and Advanced L2 Learners*. Unpublished Ph.D. thesis, Georgetown University.

Adger, C. T. (2001) 'Discourse in Educational Settings' in D. Schiffrin, D. Tannen and H. E. Hamilton (eds) *The Handbook of Discourse Analysis* (Oxford: Blackwell), pp. 503–17.

Agathopoulou, E. (2009, 7–8 February) 'Investigating the Characteristics of Successful and Unsuccessful Conference Abstracts'. Paper presented at the International Conference on Language for Specific and Academic Purposes, University of Crete.

Ainsworth-Vaughn, N. (2001) 'The Discourse of Medical Encounters' in D. Schiffrin, D. Tannen and H. E. Hamilton (eds) *The Handbook of Discourse Analysis* (Oxford: Blackwell), pp. 453–69.

Archer, D., Wilson, A. and Rayson, P. (2002) *Introduction to the USAS Category System*. Benedict Project Report October 2002. http://ucrel.lancs.ac.uk/usas, date accessed 26 January 2010.

Atherton, B. (2006) 'Balancing Needs: How Successful can a Pre-Sessional Course be?' in A. Wray and L. Gillet (eds) *Assessing the Effectiveness of EAP Programmes* (London: British Association of Lecturers in English for Academic Purposes), pp. 12–23.

Bacha, N. N. and Bahous, R. (2008) 'Contrasting Views of Business Students' Writing Needs in an EFL Environment', *English for Specific Purposes*, 27, 74–93.

Baker, P. (2006) *Using Corpora in Discourse Analysis* (London: Continuum).

Barnard, R. and Zemach, D. (2003) 'Materials for Specific Purposes' in B. Tomlinson (ed.) *Developing Materials for Language Teaching* (London: Continuum) pp. 306–23.

Basturkmen, H. (1995) *Discourse of Academic Seminars: Structures and Strategies of Interaction.* Volume 2. Unpublished PhD thesis. University of Aston in Birmingham.

Basturkmen, H. (2003) 'Specificity and ESP Course Design', *Regional English Language Council Journal*, 34, 48–63.

Basturkmen, H. (2006) *Ideas and Options in English for Specific Purposes* (Mahwah, NJ: L. Erlbaum Associates).

Basturkmen, H. (forthcoming) 'Needs Analysis and Syllabus Design for Language for Specific Purposes' in C. Chapelle (ed.) *Encyclopedia of Applied Linguistics* (Oxford: Wiley-Blackwell).

Basturkmen, H. and Bitchener, J. (2005) 'The Text and Beyond: Exploring the Expectations of the Academic Discourse Community for the Discussion of Results Section in Masters Theses', *New Zealand Studies in Applied Linguistics*, 11, 1–19.

Belcher, D. D. (2006) 'English for Specific Purposes: Teaching to Perceived Needs and Imagined Futures in Worlds of Work, Study and Everyday Life', *Teaching English to Speakers of Other Languages Quarterly*, 40, 133–56.

Bhatia, V. K. (1993) *Analysing Genre – Language Use in Professional Settings* (London: Longman).

Bhatia, V. K. (2004) *World of Written Discourse: A Genre-Based View* (London: Continuum).

Bitchener, J. (2010) *Writing an Applied Linguistics Thesis or Dissertation: A Guide to Presenting Empirical Research* (Houndmills, Basingstoke: Palgrave Macmillan).

Bitchener, J. and Basturkmen, H. (2006) 'Perceptions of the Difficulties of Postgraduate L2 Thesis Students Writing the Discussion of Results Section', *Journal of English for Academic Purposes*, 5, 4–18.

Bloor, M. and Bloor, T. (1986) *Language for Specific Purposes: Practice and Theory*, Occasional Paper Number 19 (Dublin: Trinity College).

Bolsher, S. and Smalkoski, K. (2002) 'From Needs Analysis to Curriculum Development: Designing a Course in Health-Care Communication for Immigrant Students in the USA', *English for Specific Purposes Journal*, 21, 59–79.

Burns, A. and Moore, S. (2008) 'Questioning in Simulated Accountant-Client Consultations: Exploring Implications for ESP Teaching', *English for Specific Purposes*, 27, 322–37.

Chambers, F. (1980) 'A Re-Evaluation of Needs Analysis', *English for Specific Purposes Journal*, 1, 25–33.

Chapelle, C. A. and Duff, P. A. (2003) 'Some Guidelines for Conducting Quantitative and Qualitative Research in TESOL', *Teaching English to Speakers of Other Languages Quarterly*, 37, 157–79.

Chan, C. S. C. (2009) 'Forging a Link between Research and Pedagogy: A Holistic Framework for Evaluating Business English Materials', *English for Specific Purposes*, 28, 125–36.

Cheng, A. (2006) 'Understanding Learners and Learning in ESP Genre-Based Instruction', *English for Specific Purposes*, 25, 76–89.

Cook, V. (2002) 'Language Teaching Methodology and the L2 User Perspective' in V. Cook (ed.) *Portraits of the L2 User* (Clevedon: Multilingual Matters), pp. 325–43.

Cooley, L. and Lewkowicz, J. (1995) 'The Writing Needs of Graduate Students at the University of Hong Kong: A Project Report', *Hong Kong Papers in Linguistics and Language Teaching*, 18, 121–3.

Cooley, L. and Lewkowicz, J. (1997) 'Developing Awareness of the Rhetorical and Linguistic Conventions of Writing a Thesis in English; Addressing the Needs of ESL/ EFL Postgraduate Students' in A. Duszak (ed.) *Culture and Styles of Academic Discourse* (Berlin: Mouton de Gruyter), pp. 113–40.

Cooley, L. and Lewkowicz, J. (2003) *Dissertation Writing in Practice: Turning Ideas into Text* (Hong Kong: Hong Kong University Press).

Cowling, J. D. (2007) 'Needs Analysis: Planning a Syllabus for a Series of Intensive Workplace Courses at a Leading Japanese Company', *English for Specific Purposes*, 26, 426–42.

Crandall, E. (1999) *Developing and Evaluating Pragmatics-Focused Materials*, Unpublished MA, University of Auckland.

Crandall, E. and Basturkmen, H. (2004) 'Evaluating Pragmatics Focused Materials', *English Language Teaching Journal*, 58, 38–49.

Creswell, J. W. (2003) *Research Design: Qualitative, Quantitative and Mixed Methods Approaches* (London: Sage).

Denzin, N. K. and Lincoln, Y. S. (2000) *Handbook of Qualitative Research*, 2nd edn (California: Sage).

Ding, H. (2007) 'Genre Analysis of Personal Statements: Analysis of Moves in Application Essays to Medical and Dental Schools', *English for Specific Purposes*, 26, 368–92.

Dong, Y. (1998) 'Non-Native Graduate Students' Thesis/Dissertation Writing in Science: Self Reports by Students and their Advisors from Two US Institutions', *English for Specific Purposes*, 17, 369–90.

Dudley-Evans, T. and St John, M. J. (1998) *Developments in English for Specific Purposes* (Cambridge: Cambridge University Press).

Ellis, R. (1996) 'SLA and Language Pedagogy', *Studies in Second Language Acquisition*, 19, 69–92.

Ellis, R. (2005) 'Instructed Language Learning and Task-Based Teaching' in E. Hinkle (ed.) *Handbook of Research in Second Language Teaching and Learning* (Mahwah, NJ: Lawrence Erlbaum Associates) pp. 713–28.

Evans, D. and Gruba, P. (2002) *How to Write a Better Thesis* (Melbourne, Australia: Melbourne University Press).

Ferris, D. (1998) 'Students' Views of Academic Aural/Oral Skills: A Comparative Analysis', *Teaching English to Speakers of Other Languages Quarterly*, 32, 289–318.

Ferris, D. (2001) 'Teaching Writing for Academic Purposes' in J. Flowerdew and M. Peacock (eds) *Research Perspectives in English for Academic Purposes* (Cambridge: Cambridge University Press), pp. 298–314.

Fletcher Building Annual Report (2009) *The Year in Full: Wider Perspectives* (Auckland: Fletcher Building).

Flowerdew, J. and Wan, A. (2006) 'Genre Analysis of Tax Computation Letters: How and Why do Tax Accountants Write as they do', *English for Specific Purposes*, 25, 133–53.

Friedenberg, J., Kennedy, D., Lomperis, A., Martin, W. and Westerfield, K. (2003) *Effective Practices in Workplace Language Training: Guidelines for Providers of English Language Training Services* (Alexandria, VA: Teachers of English to Speakers of Other Languages, Inc).

Garcia Mayo, M de Pilar. (2000) *English for Specific Purposes: Discourse Analysis and Course Design* (Bibao: Universidad del Pais Vasco/Euskal Heriko Unibertsitatea).

Gee, J. P. (2005) *An Introduction to Discourse Analysis: Theory and Method*, 2nd edition (London: Routledge).

Gibbons, J. (2001) 'Revising the Language of New South Wales Police Procedures: Applied Linguistics in Action', *Applied Linguistics*, 22, 439–69.

Gillet, A. and Wray, L. (2006) 'EAP and Success' in A. Gillet and L. Wray (eds) *Assessing the Effectiveness of EAP Programmes* (London: British Association of Lecturers in English for Academic Purposes), pp. 1–11.

Harding, K. (2007) *English for Specific Purposes* (Oxford: Oxford University Press).

Harrison, C. and Wood, P. (1992) *Art in Theory: 1900–1990* (Oxford: Blackwell).

Hart, C. (2005) *Doing Your Masters Dissertation* (London: Sage).

Henry, A. (2007) 'Evaluating Language Learners' Response to Web-Based, Data-Driven, Genre Teaching Materials', *English for Specific Purposes* 26, 462–84.

Hocking, D. (2004) 'The Genre of the Postgraduate Exegesis in Art and Design: An Ethnographic Examination', *Hong Kong Journal of Applied Linguistics*, 8: 54–77.

Hocking, D. and Fieldhouse, W. (2005) Academic Literacies and Subject Content: The Case of the Foundation Art and Design Theory Paper (Unpublished manuscript).

Holme, R. (1996) *ESP Ideas* (Harlow, Essex: Longman).

Holme, R. and Chalauisaeng, B. (2006) 'The Learner as Needs Analyst: The Use of Participatory Appraisal in the EAP Reading Classroom', *English for Specific Purposes*, 25, 403–19.

Holmes, J., Vine, B. and Johnson, G. (1998) *Guide to the Wellington Corpus of Spoken New Zealand English* (Wellington, New Zealand: School of Linguistics and Applied Language Studies, Victoria University of Wellington).

Howard, R. (1997) 'LSP in the UK' in R. Howard and G. Brown (eds) *Teacher Education for LSP* (Clevedon: Multilingual Matters), pp. 41–57.

Hüttner, J., Smit, U. and Mehlmauer-Larcher, B. (2009) 'ESP Teacher Education at the Interface of Theory and Practice: Introducing a Model of Mediated Corpus-Based Genre-Analysis', *System*, 37, 99–115.

Hyland, K. (2002a) 'Specificity Revisited: How Far Should We Go?' *English for Specific Purposes*, 21:4, 385–95.

Hyland, K. (2002b) *Teaching and researching writing.* (Harlow: Longman).

Hyland, K. (2003) 'Genre-Based Pedagogies: A Social Response to Process', *Journal of Second Language Writing*, 12: 17–29.

Hyland, K. (2004) *Genre and Second Language Writing* (Ann Arbor: University of Michigan Press).

Hyland, K. (2006) *English for Academic Purposes: An Advanced Resource Book* (London: Routledge).

Hyland, K. (2008) 'The Author Replies', *Teaching English to Speakers of Other Languages Quarterly*, 42, 113–4.

Hyland, K. (2009) 'Specific Purposes Programs' in M. H. Long, and C. J. Doughty (eds) *The Handbook of Language Teaching* (Oxford: Wiley Blackwell), pp. 201–17.

Jackson, L., Meyer, W. and Parkinson, J. (2006) 'The Writing Tasks and Reading Assigned to Undergraduate Science Students', *English for Specific Purposes*, 25, 260–81.

Johns, A. M. and Dudley-Evans, T. (1991) 'English for Specific Purposes: International in Scope, Specific in Purpose', *Teaching English to Speakers of Other Languages Quarterly*, 25, 297–314.

Johns, A. M. and Price-Machada, D. (2001) 'English for Specific Purposes (ESP): Tailoring Courses to Students' Needs – and to the Outside World' in M. Celce-Murcia (ed.) *Teaching English as a Second or Foreign Language*, 3rd edn (Boston: Heinle and Heinle), pp. 43–54.

Johnstone, B. (2008) *Discourse Analysis*, 2nd edn (Oxford: Blackwell).

Jordan, R. R. (1997) *English for Academic Purposes: A Guide and Resource Book for Teachers* (Cambridge: Cambridge University Press).

Kasper, L. F. (1997) 'The Impact of Content-Based Instructional Programs on the Academic Progress of ESL Students', *English for Specific Purposes*, 16, 309–20.

Kim, D. (2008) *English for Occupational Purposes: One Language?* (London: Continuum).

Kim, S. (2006) 'Academic Oral Communication Needs of East Asian International Graduate Students in Non-Science and Non-Engineering Fields', *English for Specific Purposes*, 25, 479–89.

Kumar, R. (1996) *Research Methodology: A Step-By-Step Guide for Beginners* (Melbourne: Addison Wesley Longman).

Lave, J. and Wenger, E. (1991) *Situated Learning: Legitimate Peripheral Participation* (New York: Cambridge University Press).

Lea, M. (2004) 'Academic Literacies: A Pedagogy for Course Design', *Studies in Higher Education*, 2, 739–56.

Lea, M. and Street, B. (1998) 'Student Writing in Higher Education: An Academic Literacies Approach', *Studies in Higher Education*, 23: 157–72.

Long, M. H. (2005) 'Methodological Issues in Learner Needs Analysis' in M. H. Long (ed.) *Second Language Needs Analysis* (Cambridge: Cambridge University Press), pp. 19–78.

Mackey, A. and Gass, S. M. (2005) *Second Language Research: Methodology and Design* (Mahwah, NJ: Lawrence Erlbaum Associates).

Martala, M. (2006) 'Tracking Pre-Sessional Students' Writing Abilities at the University of Hertfordshire' in A. Wray and L. Gillet (eds) *Assessing the Effectiveness of EAP Programmes* (London: British Association of Lecturers in English for Academic Purposes), pp. 40–55.

Master, P. (1997a) 'ESP Teacher Education in the USA' in R. Howard and G. Brown, (eds) *Teacher Education for LSP* (Clevedon: Multilingual Matters), pp. 22–40.

Master, P. (1997b) 'Using Models in EST', *English Teaching Forum*, 35, 4.

Master, P. (2005) 'English for Specific Purposes' in E. Hinkel (ed.) *Handbook of Research in Second Language Teaching and Learning* (Mahwah, NJ: Lawrence Erlbaum Associates), pp. 99–115.

Molle, D. and Prior, P. (2008) 'Multimodal Genre Systems in EAP Writing Pedagogy: Reflecting on a Needs Analysis', *Teaching English to Speakers of Other Languages Quarterly* 42, 541–66.

Northcott, J. (2001) 'Towards an Ethnography of the MBA Classroom: A Consideration of the Role of Interactive Lecturing Styles Within the Context of an MBA Programme', *English for Specific Purposes* 20, 15–37.

Nunan, D. (1992) *Research Methods in Language Teaching* (Cambridge: Cambridge University Press).

Nunan, D. (2004) *Task-Based Language Teaching* (Cambridge: Cambridge University Press).

Paltridge, B. (2006) *Discourse Analysis: An Introduction* (London: Continuum).

Paltridge, B. and Starfield, S. (2007) *Thesis and Dissertation Writing in a Second Language: A Handbook for Supervisors* (New York: Routledge).

Parkinson, J., Jackson, L., Kirkwood, T. and Padayachee, V. (2007) 'A Scaffolded Reading and Writing Course for Foundation Level Science Students', *English for Specific Purposes*, 26, 443–61.

Parks, S. (2001) 'Moving from School to the Workplace: Disciplinary Innovation, Border Crossings, and the Reshaping of a Written Genre', *Applied Linguistics*, 22, 405–38.

Rapley, T. (2007) *Doing Conversation, Discourse and Document Analysis* (London: Sage).

Rayson, P. (2009) *Wmatrix: a web-based corpus processing environment*, Computing Department, Lancaster University. http://ucrel.lancs.ac.uk/wmatrix/).

Richards, K. (2003) *Qualitative Inquiry in TESOL* (Houndmills, Basingstoke: Palgrave Macmillan).

Ridley, D. (2006) 'Tracking a Cohort of Pre-Sessional Students at Sheffield Hallam University' in A. Wray and L. Gillet (eds) *Assessing the Effectiveness of EAP Programmes* (London: British Association of Lecturers in English for Academic Purposes), pp. 24–39.

Roberts, C. (2005) 'English in the Workplace' in E. Hinkel (ed.) *Handbook of Research in Second Language Teaching and Learning* (Mahwah, NJ: Lawrence Erlbaum Associates), pp. 117–37.

Robinson, P. (1991) *ESP Today: A Practitioner's Guide* (Hemel Hempstead: Prentice Hall).

Roehr, K. (2007) 'Metalinguistic Knowledge and Language Ability in University-Level L2 Learners', *Applied Linguistics*, 29, 173–99.

Rudestam, K. and Newton, R. (2001) *Surviving Your Dissertation: A Comprehensive Guide to Content and Process* (Newbury Park, CA: Sage).

Samraj, B. (2002) 'Texts and Contextual Layers: Academic Writing in Content Classes' in A. Johns (ed.) *Genre in the Classroom* (Mahwah, NJ: Lawrence Erlbaum), pp. 163–76.

Song, B. (2006) 'Content-Based ESL Instruction: Long Term Effects and Outcomes', *English for Specific Purposes*, 25, 420–37.

Swales, J. (1990) *Genre Analysis: English in Academic and Research Settings* (Cambridge: Cambridge University Press).

Swales, J. (2004) *Research Genres: Exploration and Applications* (Cambridge: Cambridge University Press).

Swales, J. (2009) 'When There is no Perfect Text: Approaches to the EAP Practitioner's Dilemma', *Journal of English for Academic Purposes*, 8, 5–13.

Sysoyev, P. V. (2001) 'Developing an ESP Course: A Framework for a Learner-Centred Classroom', *The ESP Newsletter*. Issue 1.

Tajino, A., James, R. and Kijima, K. (2005) 'Beyond Needs Analysis: Soft Systems Methodology for Meaningful Collaboration in EAP Course Design', *Journal of English for Academic Purposes*, 4, 27–42.

Thomas, J. (2009) *The Language Based Tasks of Civil Engineers in a New Zealand Workplace*. MA dissertation, Department of Applied Language Studies and Linguistics, University of Auckland.

Thompson, P. (1999) 'Exploring the Contexts of Writing: Interviews with PhD Supervisors' in P. Thompson (ed.) *Issues in EAP Writing Research and Instruction* (Reading: Centre for Applied Language Studies, University of Reading), pp. 37–54.

Thompson, S. E. (2003) 'Text-Structuring Metadiscourse, Intonation and the Signalling of Organisation in Academic Lectures', *Journal of English for Academic Purposes* 2, 5–20.

Tudor, I. (1997) 'LSP or Language Education?' in R. Howard and G. Brown (eds) *Teacher Education for LSP* (Clevedon: Multilingual Matters), pp. 90–102.

Turner, J. and Hocking, D. (2004) 'Synergy in Art and Language: Positioning the Language Specialist in Contemporary Art Study', *Art and Design Communication in Higher Education* 3, 149–62.

Uvin, J. (1996) 'Designing Workplace ESOL Courses for Chinese Health-Care Workers at a Boston Nursing Home' in K. Graves (ed.) *Teachers as Course Developers* (Cambridge: Cambridge University Press), pp. 39–62.

Vygotsky, L. S. (1978) *Mind in Society: The Development of Higher Psychological Processes* (Cambridge: Harvard University Press).

Wenger, E. (1998) *Communities of Practice: Learning, Meaning and Identity* (Cambridge: Cambridge University Press).

Wenger, E., McDermott R. and Snyder, W. M. (2002) *Cultivating Communities of Practice* (Boston: Harvard Business School Press).

West, R. (1997) 'Needs Analysis: State of the Art' in R. Howard and G. Brown (eds) *Teacher Education for LSP* (Clevedon: Multilingual Matters), pp. 68–79.

Widdowson, H. (1983) *Learning Purpose and Language Use* (Oxford: Oxford University Press).

Author Index

Abbuhl, R. J., 66, 67
Adger, C. T., 38
Agathopoulou, E., 45
Ainsworth-Vaughn, N., 39
Archer, D., 47
Atherton, B., 65

Bacha, N. N., 30
Bahous, R., 30
Baker, P., 47
Barnard, R., 3
Basturkmen, H., 38, 56, 61, 67, 106, 125, 128, 129
Belcher, D. D., 56, 59, 60
Bhatia, V. K., 44
Bitchener, J., 125, 127, 128, 129, 132, 136
Bloor, M., 186
Bloor, T., 186
Bolsher, S., 29
Burns, A., 49

Chalauisaeng, B., 144
Chambers, F., 18
Chan, C. S. C., 67
Chapelle, C. A., 44
Cheng, A., 65, 66, 135
Cook, V., 7
Cooley, L., 125
Cowling, J. D., 61, 144
Crandall, E., 67
Creswell, J. W., 44

Denzin, N. K., 43
Ding, H., 46
Dong, Y., 125
Dudley-Evans, T., 9, 2, 8, 13, 18, 56, 59, 142
Duff, P. A., 44

Ellis, R., 7, 105
Evans, D., 125

Ferris, D., 27, 54
Fieldhouse, W., 115, 116, 119
Fletcher Building Annual Report, 60

Flowerdew, J., 50, 57
Friedenberg, J., 86

Garcia Mayo, M de Pilar., 17
Gass, S. M., 31, 125
Gee, J. P., 112
Gibbons, J., 39
Gillet, A., 9, 65
Gruba, P., 125

Harding, K., 63
Hart, C., 125
Henry, A., 67
Hocking, D., 111, 113, 115, 116, 119
Holme, R., 2, 144
Holmes, J., 42
Howard, R., 7
Hüttner, J., 43, 47
Hyland, K., 19, 37, 54, 55, 57, 86, 114, 119, 120, 136, 139

Jackson, L., 61
James, R., 17
Johns, A. M., 9, 33, 34, 56
Johnson, G., 42
Johnstone, B., 38
Jordan, R. R., 54

Kasper, L. F., 10, 13
Kijima, K., 17
Kim, D., 9
Kim, S., 27, 28
Kumar, R., 31, 32

Lave, J., 11
Lea, M., 109, 114, 121
Lewkowicz, J., 125
Lincoln, Y. S., 43
Long, M. H., 144

McDermott R., 11
Mackey, A., 31, 125
Martala, M., 65
Master, P., 7, 9, 10, 42, 58
Mehlmauer-Larcher, B., 43
Meyer, W., 61

Molle, D., 33
Moore, S., 49

Newton, R., 125
Northcott, J., 44
Nunan, D., 2, 31

Paltridge, B., 45, 112, 125
Parkinson, J., 61, 62
Parks, S., 37, 45
Price-Machada, D., 33, 34
Prior, P., 33

Rapley, T., 49, 50
Rayson, P., 47
Richards, K., 43, 44
Ridley, D., 65
Roberts, C., 42, 51
Robinson, P., 139
Roehr, K., 105
Rudestam, K., 125

Samraj, B., 57
Smalkoski, K., 29
Smit, U., 43
Snyder, W. M., 11
Song, B., 10, 12, 13

St John, M. J., 2, 8, 13, 18, 59, 142
Starfield, S., 125
Street, B., 114
Swales, J., 44, 63, 64
Sysoyev, P. V., 19

Tajino, A., 17
Thomas, J., 144
Thompson, P., 125
Thompson, S. E., 42
Tudor, I., 8
Turner, J., 111, 113

Uvin, J., 58

Vine, B., 42
Vygotsky, L. S., 19

Wan, A., 50, 57
Wenger, E., 11
West, R., 18
Widdowson, H., 58
Wilson, A., 47
Wray, L., 9, 65

Zemach, D., 3

Subject Index

A

academic literacies, 61, 108–121
academic skills:
  general, 53–4, 74
  listening, 20–21, 27, 30, 41–2, 44, 52,
    140
  reading, 4, 5, 10, 12, 18, 21, 30, 41,
    61–3, 110, 116, 121
  speaking, 8–9, 20–2, 27–8, 30, 41, 44,
    67
  writing, 4–6, 12, 20, 21–3, 25, 30–1,
    41, 47, 50, 54–5, 57, 61, 64–7, 74,
    108–120, 122–135, 141–3
academic success, *see also* evaluation, 21,
  27–8, 65, 74
academic vocabulary, 31, 41, 54, 57, 125
activities,
  based on authentic texts, 49, 52, 60,
    62–4, 68,
  choices for instruction, 2, 5, 13, 18–9,
    59, 86, 98, 102, 107, 131, 142–3
aims of ESP teaching, 3, 7–8, 11, 68,
  142
analysing needs, *see also* needs analysis,
  17–35, 137, 143–4
appropriacy of language use, 8, 29, 67,
  73, 93, 97, 102, 107, 114,
  129–130
areas of ESP teaching, 3–6, 12
authentic and non authentic texts, 49, 52,
  60, 62–4, 68
awareness, 9, 42, 66–7, 76, 92, 104, 113,
  115, 125, 135

B

background knowledge, 12, 110
beliefs and interests of teachers, 19, 56,
  86, 112, 139
branches of ESP, 6, 39
branches of work and study, 5–55, 57, 141
business English, 3–4, 30, 38, 46, 53–5,
  61, 67
  accountancy, 50, 53, 55, 63

  management, 5, 53–6
  marketing, 53–4, 56
business meetings, 61, 67

C

carrier and real content, 52, 59–62, 68
characteristics of ESP, 13, 62
communication skills, 12, 17, 33, 53, 84,
  89–90, 101, 103, 142
community of practice, 11–12, 37, 142–3
communicative competence, 7
content-based instruction, 5, 10–12, 61
conceptual knowledge, 9, 139, 143
conceptual content in the syllabus, 7–8,
  61, 104, 108, 110–11, 120–1, 139,
  142–3
concordances, 47–8, 79–80
constraints, 9, 18–19, 84–5, 104–5,
  118–19, 131–5
consultations
  medical, 88–106, 138–9, 140–2
  with accountants, 49–50
context, 3–5, 8, 19, 71–72, 89–90,
  109–110, 123–4, 137, 140
corpora, 42, 47, 49, 50–51, 75, 77,
  79–80, 84, 86, 140, 142–3
corporate confidentiality, 9
corpus analysis, 36, 43, 46–7, 137, 139
cost, 9, 59
course objectives, 65, 76
course timing, 6, 86, 106, 135
critical function of writing, 113, 115–9
cultural content in the syllabus, 18, 29,
  61, 90, 143

D

demands of teaching ESP, 1, 7–9
descriptions of specialist discourse, 8, 12,
  19, 36–49
  published descriptions, 42–3, 46, 49,
    51, 53–4, 56–7, 85, 94, 105, 114,
    140, 143
difficulties, *see under* constrains

154

disciplinary knowledge, *see under* conceptual knowledge
discipline-specific EAP (ESAP), 6, 8, 114, 120, 141
discourse community, 36, 44–6, 58, 66–7, 127, 129, 136
discussion skills, 9, 20–2, 25–8, 34
document analysis, 44, 50–1
during-experience ESP, *see also* experience of learners, 6, 56, 108

E

effectiveness of ESP, 9–12, 64–6, 135
English for academic purposes, EGAP and ESAP distinction, 6
English for care home workers, 24–5, 28–30, 32–3
English for engineering: 3, 4, 9, 144
English for finance, 4, 56, 59
English for general academic purposes (EGAP), 6, 8, 41, 53–4, 60
English for healthcare, 6, 29–30, 53–4, 90
English for the hospitality industry, 61
English for lawyers, 4–6, 66, 73
English for medical doctors, 88–107
English for nursing, 6, 8, 29–30, 37, 45, 54, 63
English for the police, 71–87
English for occupational purposes (EOP), 5, 7–8, 53, 58
EGOP and ESOP distinction, 6
English for professional purposes (EPP), 5–6, 8, 11, 13, 17–18, 40, 56–8, 65, 71–87, 88–107,
EGPP and ESPP distinction, 6
English for specific academic purposes, ESAP and EGAP distinction, 6, 108–121
English for thesis writing, 122–136
English for visual arts studies, 108–121
English Language Teaching (ELT), *also* general English language teaching, 1–3, 7–8, 9, 13, 61
error correction, *see also* feedback, 102
experience
  of learners, 6, 18, 66, 139
    during-experience ESP, 6, 56
    pre-experience ESP, 6, 11, 56, 72, 108
    post-experience ESP, 6, 12, 56, 90, 104
  of teachers, 7–8, 85, 89, 126, 139

ethnography, 36, 43–4, 49–50, 137, 142
evaluation
  courses, 22, 64–6, 124, 135
  learning, *see also* effectiveness of ESP, 84
  materials, 67

F

feedback to learners, 22–23, 66–7, 84, 91, 93, 95, 98, 101–2, 110, 121, 137
functions of language, 60

G

generic skills: 54, 56, 58
genres
  conference abstracts, 44–5, 64, 126, 129
  discussions of results, 124, 126, 127–9
  literature reviews, 64, 123–124, 126, 129, 131–4
  nursing care plans, 37, 44–5, 63
  office legal memoranda, 66
  personal statements, 46
genre analysis, 18, 23, 33, 36, 43, 44–6, 50, 140
  move anlaysis, 46, 110, 119, 126–133, 136
genre-based writing instruction, *see also* English for thesis writing, 136
goals of learners, 7–8
grammar, 13, 60, 66, 68, 76, 102, 125
grouping students, 53

H

hedging, *see also* tentative uses of language, 95–7

I

Immigrants, 4, 89
informants, *also* insider-experts, 7, 27, 140
interviews, 29–30. 31, 33, 44, 50, 65, 121, 127–8, 137, 142–3, 144
instructional materials, 10, 37, 41, 52, 62–4, 67–8, 76–83, 97–104, 114–8, 129–131, 142–4
instructional strategy, 101–102
investigating needs, *also* needs analysis, 17–35, 72–4, 90–2, 110–11, 124–6, 137, 139

investigating specialist discourse, 36–51,
74–6, 92–7, 111–4, 126–9, 137,
139–140

J

job shadowing, 33, 50

K

knowledge (linguistic)
implicit, 105
explicit, 76
metalinguistic, 104, 105

L

legal discourse, 5, 67
language
use, *see also* descriptions of specialist
discourse, 8, 9, 12, 18, 19, 21, 23,
30, 32–34, 36–49, 52–9, 61, 63, 131,
138, 141,145,
usage, 8
skills, 5, 11, 30, 32, 53, 59, 76, 90–1,
94
varieties, 53, 94
learner factor analysis, 19, 21, 34
learning through content, *see under*
content-based instruction
learning styles, 23
linguistic analysis, 18
literature review, *see under* genres

M

motivation, 11,19
means analysis, 18–19
medical discourse, 104–5
methodology in teaching, 13, 86, 142
mixed disciplines of students, 64, 123
moves, *see under* genre analysis
multiple methods in needs analysis,
30, 61

N

narrative accounts, 44, 75
narrow angled course design, *see also* wide
angled, 52–9, 68, 137, 141,
143

needs, 2–4, 13, 17–35
immediate/long term, 85, 141, 143
learning, 18
objective/subjective, 18
needs analysis
pre-course and on-going, 26
present situation analysis, 18, 19, 22,
98, 138
target situation analysis, *also* analysis
of objective needs, 17–19, 20, 22,
26, 30, 32–4, 39, 41, 57–8,
98, 106–8, 138, 140, 142,
144
task based, 138, 144
types of information to collect, 30–4
non authentic texts, *see under* authentic
and non authentic texts
notions, 61

O

observation
in needs analysis, 25, 29, 33, 44,
144
of spoken interaction, 30, 67, 75, 77,
90–5, 140
occuptional purposes, *see under* English
for Occupational Purposes
on-site courses, 5, 7, 143

P

performance
of students,10, 22, 29, 30, 32–4, 89, 91,
93, 98, 101, 102–4, 143
post-experience ESP, *see under* experience
of learners
postgraduate students, 4, 56–7, 66, 121,
123, 138
pre-experience ESP, *see under* experience
of learners
prefabricated chunks of language, 103
present situation analysis, 18–9, 22,
138
pre-sessional EAP, 65–6
primary data, 26, 40, 49, 143
professional purposes or English for
professional purposes (EPP), 5–6,
71–86, 88–107
proficiency, 3, 10, 18, 23, 53, 56–7, 73,
84, 89–90
pronunciation, 24–5, 27, 29,73, 105

Q

qualitative research, 43–4, 125
questionnaires, 27–34, 65–7, 137

R

real content, *see under* carrier content
recordings of spoken interaction, *see also*
     observations of spoken interaction,
     94, 42, 49, 98, 102, 105, 140,
     142
relative importance of needs, 20
refining course content, 17, 19, 25–6
register, *see also* language varieties, 13, 55,
     73, 76
requests, *see under* speech acts
role play, *also* simulations, 24, 49, 90–3,
     95, 98, 101–2, 139

S

Scaffolding, 62
scientific discourse, 54, 113
situated language use, 8
sociocultural theory, 62
study-related ESP, *see under* English for
     Academic Purposes
single discipline EAP, *see under* English for
     Academic Purposes, EGAP and ESAP
     distinction
specificity, *see also* narrow and wide
     angled course design, 37, 54–5, 57,
     107, 119, 141
speaking events
   academic juries, 41
   discussions, 20–1, 27–8
   police cautions, 39
   tutorials, 40, 75–7
   See also medical consultations
speech acts
   questions, 38–40
   requests, 39, 67
strategies (learning), 36, 61, 76
spoken discourse, *also* spoken
     interaction, 39, 42, 45, 74–5, 140,
     142–3
stakeholders, 84
subject specialists, *see also* insider experts,
     106–8, 120–1
success, *see under* evaluation
surveys, 21, 27–8, 30
syllabus, 2, 22, 37, 59–61, 68, 142–3

T

target situation analysis, *see under* needs
     analysis
tasks, *also* real-world task, 2–3, 18–9, 30,
     33–4, 61, 63, 86, 138, 143–4
teacher education, 7, 43, 85–6
teachers' values and interests, *see under*
     beliefs
team teaching, 121
technical vocabulary, 25, 74, 142
tentative uses of language, *see also* hedges:
     97
text analysis, *see also* genre analysis *and*
     corpus analysis, 2–3, 43, 127, 130,
     143–4
transfer of skills and knowladge, 54–5,
     135

U

undergraduate students, 20
up skilling, 90, 95

V

varieties, *see under* language varieties
vocabulary
   collocations, 47, 59, 73, 76, 84, 142
   core, 54, 56
   formulaic expressions, 103–4
   single and multi-word units, 142
   See also concordances *and* technical
     vocabulary
vocational ESP, *see under* English for
     Occupational Purposes

W

wants (in needs analysis), 18
web-based materials, 67, 71, 142
wide-angled course design, *see also* narrow
     angled, 3, 53–6, 60
work-related ESP, *see under* English for
     Occultional Purposes and English
     for Professional Purposes
writing as performance, 112–3

Z

zone of proximal development, 19